Baubles, Buttons and Beads

The Heritage of Bohemia

Sibylle Jargstorf

Schiffer Publishing Ltd

77 Lower Valley Road, Atglen, PA 19310

Acknowledgements

The most enriching experience in conceiving this book has been meeting the many wonderful people who share my interests and enthusiasm.

My very special thanks go to the many Gablonzers who never tired of answering my questions, including: Emil Elstner, Emil and Erna Jantsch, Karl Posselt, Ernst and Maria Seidel and Max Stecker. I owe as much to the kind cooperation of Susanne Rössler and Dr. Gertrud Zasche, curators of the Glass and Jewelry Museum in Neugablonz.

The knowledge I have compiled would have been plain and colorless without the help of Joan Bygrave and Elizabeth Spilstead in London. They found the most valuable reference pieces for me.

I will appreciate forever having met them all. I am thankful not only for the facts that they allowed me to find, but also for the kindness and generosity they allowed me to see.

Also by Sibylle Jargstorf:

Glass in Jewelry
Paperweights

Published by Schiffer Publishing Ltd.
77 Lower Valley Road
Atglen, PA 19310
Please write for a free catalog.
This book may be purchased from the publisher.
Please include $2.95 postage.
Try your bookstore first.

Contents

Foreword

This book deals with the production of jewelry ("bijouterie") and other glass trinkets in the town of Gablonz and its outskirts. Worldwide, the name "Gablonz" was once the keyword of quality among the makers of costume jewelry. Most renowned manufacturers (such as Coro, Miriam Haskell and Trifari) got their jewelry or the elements for their jewelry from the Gablonz craftsmen and workshops. Still, hardly any of those who admired and wore costume jewelry knew about the eminent role of the Gablonzers, since their names were never attached to the finished pieces.

While American consumers may not have been previously aware of their Bohemian benefactors, their impact on American jewelry fashion was tremendous. Reciprocally, the American market was crucial to the expansion of the Bohemian industry. The following figures should convey the scale of the interaction between these two partners in trade:

Bohemian export to the United States, 1920-1930

	tons	% of Bohemian output
Beads	41,704	35.4%
Buttons	11,298	37.5%
Stones	3,253	39.0%
Bijouterie	108,222	30.0%

(Prediger, 1932, pp. 16-19)

The tides of European history, World War I, World War II and increasing industrialization have taken a tragic toll on the history and the heritage of the skilled craftsmen of Gablonz; they are gone, and their past is nearly forgotten. This book tries to retrace their development, and to illustrate how extensive and exquisite a selection of jewelry the Gablonzers once offered the world for our continuing pleasure and adornment.

Baubles, Buttons & Beads:
The People

The town of Gablonz can be found on the northern fringe of Bohemia. Bohemia lies in the very heart of Europe. Its social and cultural identity developed over about ten centuries — from the tenth up to the first half of the twentieth century, when it was inhabited by Czech and German Bohemians. Its central position and the periods of peaceful competition between those two ethnic groups made a stable, flourishing economy possible, though of course there were disruptions.

Bohemia's prosperity was radically disturbed for the first time during the Husite Wars, from 1419 to 1436. The Gablonz area had been used peacably by Czech, Frankonian and Thuringian farmers since the twelvth century, but the Husite Wars left the region devastated and depopulated. After the wars, the landlords of the territory — the Wartenbergers — decided to attract German craftsmen and merchants to their lands, to improve the economic structure of their fiefs.

The Wartenbergers invited textile makers from neighboring Reichenberg and attracted glass-makers from Southern Germany and Saxonia. This drew the Schürer, Wander and Preissler (Preussler) families as well, and within a few decades they had founded about a dozen successful glassworks. These attracted other glass-makers and glass-refiners from adjacent areas known for their glass-making, including Silesia, Saxonia and Bavaria. The churchbell of Gablonz, cast in 1590, was inscribed with such names as Preissler, Weyss (Weiss), Wander, Myller (Müller) and Wünsch, founding families which were eventually to become leading glass-making dynasties. Their work contributed to the worldwide reputation of Gablonz until the twentieth century.

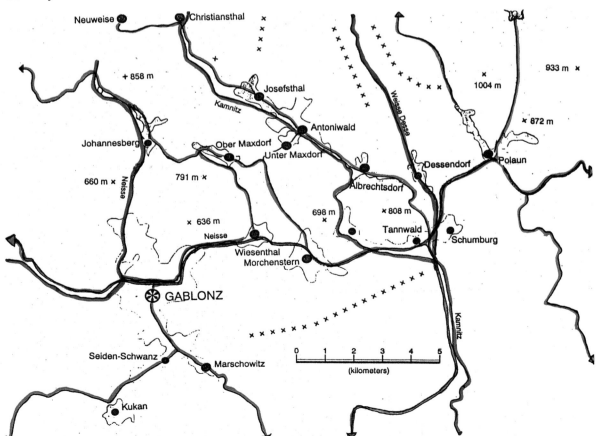

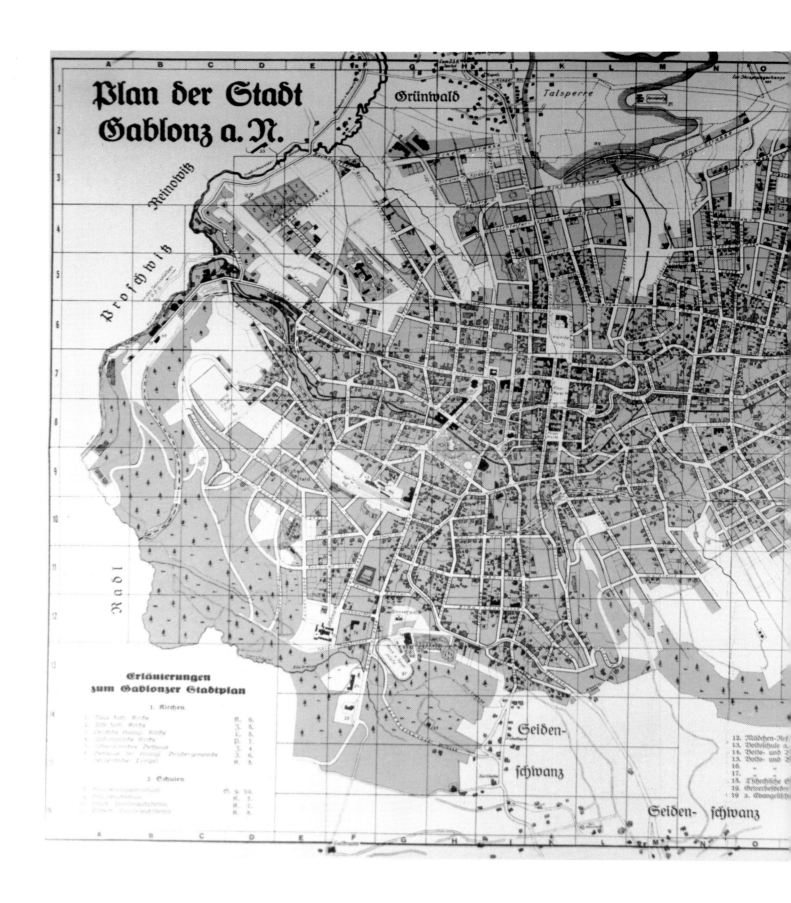

A map of Gablonz.

By 1500, the villages destroyed in the Husite Wars had been rebuilt, and Gablonz had grown into a village with 65 houses; glass and textile manufacturing had brought prosperity into this rather remote corner of Bohemia. The prosperity of all of Bohemia was further ensured when Emperor Rudolf II (1552-1612) made Prague and Bohemia the cultural centers of his monarchy, competing with the splendor of the nearby Saxonian court.

This peaceful period ended abruptly in 1618, with the onset of the 30-Years War. Beginning apparently as as conflict between religious factions, it was in reality "a gigantic duel between Austria and Spain on one hand and France, Sweden and the maritime powers on the other, with Germany the arena in which their struggle for mastery was played out."[i] The ravages of the 30-Years War left Bohemia (which had a population of about 3 million in 1618) with only 780,000 inhabitants. Of its 18,000 villages, only 5000 remained in existence.

In the early 17th century, the area around the Gablonz became part of the duchy Friedland, belonging to Albrecht von Waldstein — better known as "Wallenstein," by which name he was immortalized in Friedrich Schiller's story of his prominence and tragic end. Wallenstein was murdered, after which the area was donated (in 1634) to the count Niklas DesFours, as a reward for his loyal service to Emperor Ferdinand II. The DesFours remained the nominal landlords of the area until the end of the Habsburg Empire. Like the Wartenbergs, the DesFours sought out a new generation of pioneers to settle in the area — more families destined to determine the future of Gablonz.

The amazing continuity of Gablonz's leading families becomes obvious when the names inscribed in the 1648 land registry are compared to those dominating Gablonz directories of the late 19th and early 20th centuries.[2] In 1648 the names of tremendous dynasty families can already be found, from Bergmann, Dressler, Endler, Feix, Pilz and Posselt to Reckziegel, Rössler, Scheibler, Simm, Ulbrich, Unger and Zappe. These same names fill the pages of directories 250 years later, where a single dynasty (such as the Rösslers) is represented by fifty individual entries.

Terminology

Modern maps show only the Czech names for villages in the Gablonz area. Here is a comparison:

German	Czech
Albrechtsdorf	Albrechtice
Antoniwald	Antonínov
Christiansthal	Kristiíanov
Gablonz	Jablonec
Johannesberg	Janov
Josephsthal	Josefův Dů
Kamnitz	Kamenice
Klein-Iser	Jižerka
Kukan	Kokonín
Labau	Hut
Morchenstern	Smrzkovka
Neuwiese	Nova Louka
Polaun	Polubný
Radl	Rádlo
Reichenau	Rýchnov
Reinowitz	Rynovice
Seidenschwanz	Vrkoslaviče
Tannwald	Tanvald
Weisenthal	Lučany

The names of these manufacturing families, the backbone of Gablonz's industry, never gained renown outside the borders of their own areas, because Gablonz products were never marketed under the local makers' names. Instead, they were used in jewelry pieces sold by outside companies, who incorporated the Gablonz glass elements into their own products; these products were then marketed under the outside companies' names, not under the names of the Gablonz craftsmen. Only one Gablonz family name ever became known around the world, though not for jewelry or glass-making — the name of the family "Porsche". The designer of the famous car could trace his origins back to the Gablonz area, where the name Porsche can be found from the early 18th century on.

Gablonz and its neighboring villages grew rapidly in the second half of the 17th century. The chronicler reports in 1687, "The village Gablonitz is most conveniently situated on the road connecting Reichenberg to Zittau [both important trading cities]. It would certainly be a great advantage for the landlords if further craftsmen and traders would settle there".[3]

The DesFours realized this advantage and founded a series of new villages near Gablonz. Thus, once again the landlords and craftsmen joined forces to initiate a manufacturing economy on those arid and mountainous grounds. Such improvements of the economic infrastructure eventually made North Bohemia the leading region for the Habsburg Monarchy's economy.

Even if the Gablonz area owed its reputation mainly to the glass and jewelry industry, it was the textile industry which had largely supported the region's first economic rise. Textiles remained very important throughout Gablonz's history. The Riedel company, for example, had a world-wide reputation for high-quality glass, but also included three textile factories.

In the early 19th century, only 2000 people lived in the village of Gablonz itself, but that number cannot give an accurate idea of the town's real development. Nearly 10,000 people from the outlying regions were already cooperating in the Gablonz glass and jewelry industry, some full-time, others only part-time.

In the second half of the 19th century the population of Gablonz rose drastically. One historian wrote that "the area of Gablonz became the Austrian California. Many foreigners came to seek their fortune in the Gablonz industry and the population of Gablonz rose within the period 1857-1869 from 4553 inhabitants to 6752 inhabitants."[4] This was just the beginning of an important economic and demographic expansion.

Around 1898, the area of Gablonz counted 339 inhabitants per square kilometer, among the most densely populated sections of Bohemia. The town reflected the wealth of its 21,000 citizens, who had cooperated to equip their Gablonz with an infrastructure that many larger cities envied it. The gasworks (founded in 1872), the electricity works (1891), the impressive theater (1907), the indoor swimming pool (1908) and Bohemia's finest gymnasium (1898) were all initiated and financed by the citizens, only later to be taken over by the town's administration. The citizens put just as much effort into developing their educational system. They provided Gablonz with all the necessary schools, including not only two colleges but also the Technical Scool of the Arts (founded in 1870) and the Economical Academy (1891), a high school for business and economics.

Portrait of Franziska Hübner (1825-1899), who belonged to a renowed glass-making family that had settled in the Gablonz area in the 17th century. (Courtesy of the Museum Neugablonz)

Gablonz in 1848 and in 1888. *(Courtesy of the Museum Neugablonz)*

Jewelry made in the Technical School of Arts and Crafts, Gablonz, 1880s.

The enormously public-spirited activities of the citizens received no support from the Monarchy's central administration. Thus the first railroad crossing the area since 1859, connecting Berlin to Vienna, included no link to Gablonz, despite the economic significance of the area for the entire Monarchy, and despite the glass-makers' need for transport facilties. In 1888, the local manufacturers and exporters finally had to finance a private connecting line between Gablonz and Reichenberg. In 1850, the first important road to be built connecting Silesia and Bohemia across the Riesengebirge had similarly bypassed Gablonz.*

In large cosmopolitan cities like Prague, German-speaking Bohemians and Czech-speaking Bohemians had mingled over the centuries, but in areas on the fringes of Bohemia (like Gablonz) the two ethnic groups had maintained their own geographically distinct communities. For Gablonz, this separation had not impeded cooperation. Gablonz and its neighboring villages were inhabited by German-speaking Bohemians, while the village of Zeleny Brod — 15 km south, on the other side of the "Schwartzbrunn" mountain ridge — became the focal point of a Czech-speaking complement.** Up to the mid-19th century, both ethnic groups had contributed to the fame and wealth of Bohemia with a common "Bohemian" patriotism. Cities like Prague are the splendid products of their best creative cooperation.

However, the wave of nationalism that swept Europe in the 19th century also affected Bohemia, splitting the country into "Czech Bohemians" and "German Bohemians". Traumatized by the Austrian rule, the Czech majority in the crownland of Bohemia fought to assert Czech identity throughout Bohemia. In reaction, German Bohemians accentuated their own ancestry. By the late 19th century, the tensions and confrontation had reached such an extent that "Czech and Germans (in Bohemia) are at their wits end and act now out of nothing but national fanaticism and self-defense"[5] Frustration dictated political action for both sides of the dispute.

---

* The economic significance of the Gablonz industry rose to incredible heights in the late 19th century and the early years of the 20th. In 1911, Gablonz paid nearly 2 million Austrian Crowns in taxes to the Habsburg monarchy in Vienna - more than an entire crownland like Dalmatia could contribute to the central administration. In 1928 the Gablonzers, representing hardly more than 0.5% of the Czechoslovakian population, were responsible for more than 5% of the Republic's export business.

** In 1897, the official registry tallied the number of taxpaying glass and jewelry manufacturers in Bohemia. In German-speaking regions (Reichenberg, Friedland, Tannwald and Gablonz) there were 2104. In Czech-speaking regions (Turnov, Železny Brod, Dolni, Rokytniče and Vysoké) there were a total of 142. The Czech were primarily bead-makers (60 of them) and glass-cutters (30), and there were 25 glass agents in Turnov. These agents themselves did not produce, but organized the production and delivery of desired articles to exporters. (Tayenthal, 1900, pp. 247-250)

Gablonz a. N. Blick vom Schützenhaus

Building of the Klaar company, Gablonz. This company originated in Berlin, and moved to Gablonz in 1862 to become one of the area's leading export houses. *(Courtesy of the Museum Neugablonz)*

The family of glass-maker Josef Jantsch, from Ober-Johannesberg. The Jantsches can trace their roots in Gablonz back to the early 1700s. *(Courtesy of the Museum Neugablonz)*

A general view of Gablonz, circa 1900.

The "Gebirgsstrasse" in Gablonz, circa 1900. The solid buildings of the town reflect its wealth.

"Schwarzbrunnwarte" on top of the mountains southeast of Gablonz, before World War I.

A postcard commemorating the important 1906 exhibition in Reichenberg, near Gablonz. Feelings of nationalism began to grow in the mid-19th century, dividing Bohemians into Czech- and German-speaking factions. Because of this discord, they stopped celebrating their cultural and economic achievements as the work of one people.

The achievements of the Gablonz industry represented at the Reichenberg exhibition.

The proud presentation of the Gablonzers at the Reichenberg exhibition, held while the Emperor Franz Josef I visited.

After World War I, the Gablonz area became part of the newly founded Czechoslovakian Republic, which comprised a population of 6.7 million Czech, 3.2 million Sudetengermans (as German Bohemians were called beginning in the early 20th century), 2 million Slovaks and several other minorities. Tragically, the new Czech administration repeated the mistakes of the Habsburg monarchy. They refused to allow the kind of autonomy that holds Switzerland together so successfully, even though the first Czech president, Masaryk, had in fact promised to make his country a "second Switzerland." Instead the central government imposed Czech control on every region, placing special economic burdens on the Sudetengerman areas.***

*** After 1918, the glass and bijouterie industry in the Czech-speaking areas was considerably strengthened by support from the central administration, including the building of a School of Glassmaking in Železny Brod.

Josef Pfeiffer Strasse 34, Gablonz.

As long as business boomed, the complex of frustrations imposed by the adminisration had no major political effects. When the depression came, however, it hit Bohemia's industrialized fringes like Gablonz much harder than it did the central agricultural area. Nationalists and Hitler knew how to make skillful use of the despair caused by unemployment, and of the discontent caused by the Prague administration's missteps. Inch by inch, the Gablonzers were crushed between Czech and German nationalisms.

When the Sudetengerman parts of Czechoslovakia were annexed to the Reich in 1938, most Gablonzers dreamed that they had finally achieved the self-determination which they had claimed in vain in 1918. They soon realized that they had been misused.

The first victims were the Socialdemocrats and the Gablonzers of Jewish origin. In 1930, 900 Jews lived in Gablonz,[6] many of whom owned renowned export houses — such as Jakob H. Jeiteles, founded in 1866, or Schindler & Co., which had sucessfully represented the Gablonz industry at the Paris World Fair in 1878. Fortunately, most of the Gablonz Jews were able to escape Nazi persecution through their close links to foreign countries.

Shaken by the depression, many manufacturers and exporters had hoped desperately that their inclusion into the large market of the Reich would save them. They soon realized what it really meant. Nazi persecution of the Jews was answered by a total boycott of their American and Jewish customers. Thus they lost their most important markets. The money conversion imposed by the Reich was very much to their disadvantage. The professional bijouterie organizations had to be dissolved, and were subordinated to the organizations based in Pforzheim and Berlin. The entire bijouterie industry was officially belittled as a "trinket" industry by the Nazi officials, and eventually many factories were converted to the production of military goods.

The Gablonzers were stunned by the final and hardest blow, now inposed by the Czech administration. In 1945/1946, 3 million Sudetengermans were expropriated and expelled. Around Gablonz, an era of glass- and jewelry-making came to a tragic end.

Necklaces made in the Technical School of Arts and Crafts, Gablonz, circa 1930.

Das Schwarze Korps

ZEITUNG DER SCHUTZSTAFFELN DER NSDAP

Organ der Reichsführung SS

Einzelpreis 15 Rpf.

Berlin, 1. Juni 1939
22. Folge · 5. Jahrgang

Schluß mit der Mumpitzindustrie

Headlines from the Nazi press. The bijouterie industry was openly scorned and discredited by "experts" in the Ministry of Economics and in the Nazi publications as a frivolous "trinket industry." They were considered decadent, and their jewelry was thought to be unfit adornment for German women.

From the early 1940s, a pressmolded pendant manufactured in Gablonz for a winter charity collection held by the Nazis in Germany. Many Gablonz makers were reduced to producing insignificant articles like this.

Notification of the expulsion and expropriation, 1946. Such notices gave 3 million Sudetengermans one day's notice that they had to evacuate Bohemia. The letters stated that they were to leave the keys to their houses and workshops with the newly-installed Czech authorities, and that they were forbidden to take any valuables with them.

Artificial gemstones from the modern-day Schuhmeier workshop, Neugablonz. The rise of the bijouterie industry in the Gablonz area started with the production of exceptional "gemstones" made with imagination, stupendous craftmanship, and little bits of simple glass.

Baubles, Buttons & Beads:
The Industry

The glass-makers and the merchants of the Isermountains implemented their own distinctive glass-making techniques during the second half of the 18th century to make pendants, artificial stones and stoppers for perfume bottles. Such articles had long since been made elsewhere; Muranese craftsmen had been making artificial gemstones since the 14th century, and France had a quasi-monopoly on pendant manufacturing. It was their new and unique methods for making the items that allowed the Bohemians to become the decisive leaders in producing small glass and glass bijouterie items starting in the mid-19th century.

The Bohemian glass-makers did not cast their pendants, as was customary in France, nor did they cut their gemstones from bits of broken glass, as was done elsewhere in imitation of the handling of natural gemstones. Instead, they used molding tongs to pressmold those articles from glass canes, which were reheated just enough to render the glass malleable. After they squeezed the items into raw shapes, different craftsmen cut and polished them into a more finalized form; the pieces could then be further refined by gilding and enameling.

The Gablonz industry was started by the daring of glass-making pioneers; they were highly inventive in accepting and implementing "revolutionary" methods for handling their unequalled range of fine glass and composition (in particular, their experimental attitude initiated the development of pressed glass). Still, the great importance the industry eventually assumed was due to several other critical factors.

—The Gablonz makers worked continuously in close cooperation with the area's metalworking craftsmen to improve their techniques and tools.
—The isolation of these skilled makers, so far away from the markets for their goods, produced complementary dynasties of versatile merchants to support the makers' efforts.
—The makers and the merchants joined forces in a unique network of multiple cooperation structures.

Silver shirtbuttons set with foiled paste; the stones and the mount may be from the Gablonz/Turnau area, 18th century. Shirtbuttons like these belong to the traditional costume jewelry (*Trachtenschmuck*) worn by European men to hold the collars of linen shirts. The stones on these buttons were cut from broken composition, not pressmolded as they would be later, after more sophisticated techniques were invented.

Blown "pearls" from Gablonz, early 20th century. "Fish-silver lined" pearl beads like these were blown in the area starting in the 18th century.

Glasfabriken — In den Gemeinden	Ende 1860	Ende 1865	Ende 1870	Ende 1873	Ende 1876
Josefsthal	—	2	1	1	2
Polaun	1	1	2	2	2
Summa	1	3	3	3	4

Buchbinder und Cartonuelmacher

In den Gemeinden	Ende 1860	Ende 1865	Ende 1870	Ende 1873	Ende 1876
Gablonz	5	11	18	16	24
Grünwald	1	—	2	2	3
Maxdorf	—	—	—	—	1
Johannesberg	—	—	—	1	—
Wiesenthal	—	1	1	1	—
Neudorf	—	—	—	—	2
Kukan	—	—	1	2	1
Josefsthal	—	—	—	—	1
Labau	—	—	—	1	2
Morchenstern	—	2	—	6	3
Polaun	—	—	—	—	1
Prichowitz	—	—	2	3	1
Summa	6	14	24	32	39

Glashändler und Exporteure — In den Gemeinden	Ende 1860	Ende 1865	Ende 1870	Ende 1873	Ende 1876
Gablonz	31	32	59	58	59
Grünwald	6	4	5	5	6
Johannesberg	3	2	1	—	2
Josefsthal	3	—	—	—	6
Maxdorf	9	3	6	2	—
Wiesenthal	22	23	25	18	10
Neudorf	11	15	11	11	11
Kukan	7	14	10	8	3
Marschowitz	1	2	5	3	14
Labau	2	2	2	3	15
Nadl	—	—	—	—	3
Dalleschitz	2	2	—	1	1
Puletschnei	—	2	—	1	1
Reichenau	6	13	16	16	12
Morchenstern	27	19	21	16	12
Albrechtsdorf	16	7	8	8	38
Tannwald	4	7	7	8	9
Schumburg	1	—	—	1	—
Prichowitz	4	2	3	3	2
Polaun	5	—	5	5	9
Summa	160	155	185	167	203

Oehlmaler und Dosenerzeuger

In der Gemeinde	Ende 1860	Ende 1865	Ende 1870	Ende 1873	Ende 1876
Reichenau	20	8	12	19	40

Glascompositionsbrennereien — In den Gemeinden	Ende 1856	Ende 1860	Ende 1865	Ende 1870	Ende 1873	Ende 1876
Gablonz	4	9	7	6	4	4
Grünwald	—	3	—	—	—	2
Reinowitz	1	1	1	3	1	—
Johannesberg	1	2	1	1	—	—
Josefsthal	9	14	7	7	5	6
Maxdorf	1	11	4	—	—	—
Wiesenthal	6	4	8	4	4	10
Neudorf	5	4	5	3	2	3
Kukan	—	1	4	1	1	1
Morchenstern	6	35	9	7	9	2
Albrechtsdorf	5	18	10	12	14	2
Tannwald	—	4	1	1	—	—
Summa	38	106	57	45	40	31

Glas- und Porzellainmaler

In den Gemeinden	Ende 1856	Ende 1860	Ende 1865	Ende 1870	Ende 1873	Ende 1876
Gablonz	1	8	5	12	12	31
Reinowitz	—	—	—	—	—	1
Grünwald	—	1	—	3	2	7
Johannesberg	1	1	1	—	—	3
Maxdorf	—	—	1	1	—	3
Wiesenthal	7	5	12	13	20	30
Neudorf	2	3	2	2	3	2
Kukan	—	1	—	2	1	—
Dalleschitz	—	—	—	—	—	—
Morchenstern	—	4	—	—	1	5
Albrechtsdorf	—	—	1	—	—	—
Prichowitz	—	2	—	—	—	8
Summa	11	25	23	33	40	88

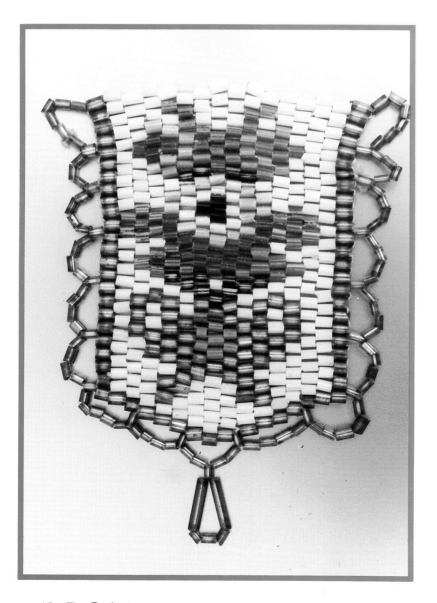

Beadwork assembled from drawn beads (*Sprengperlen*) in Gablonz, 19th century. Fairly standard, drawn beads like these were made from colored glass and/or lined with paint. They began to be produced in the area in the late 18th century, but were more or less replaced by porcelain beads in the 1880s.

Gürtlerwerkstätten							Glasspinner= und Perlblasereien							Glasbrnckereien							Glasschleifereien						
In den Gemeinden	Ende 1856	Ende 1860	Ende 1865	Ende 1870	Ende 1873	Ende 1876	In den Gemeinden	Ende 1856	Ende 1860	Ende 1865	Ende 1870	Ende 1873	Ende 1876	In den Gemeinden	Ende 1856	Ende 1860	Ende 1865	Ende 1870	Ende 1873	Ende 1876	In den Gemeinden	Ende 1856	Ende 1860	Ende 1865	Ende 1870	Ende 1876	Ende 1876
Gablonz	69	78	69	91	102	145	Gablonz	34	40	55	54	83	88	Gablonz	2	3	5	13	11	9	Gablonz	19	13	2	6	5	4
Grünwald	14	19	24	23	20	25	Grünwald	6	5	14	11	8	9	Grünwald	2	—	5	11	11	11	Grünwald	3	6	5	5	3	3
Reinowitz	—	2	2	4	3	4	Johannesberg	—	—	2	3	2	3	Reinowitz	1	—	—	1	1	—	Johannesberg	10	14	14	19	20	27
Johannesberg	—	—	—	2	1	2	Josefsthal	5	7	3	10	9	8	Johannesberg	—	—	10	16	7	10	Josefsthal	18	17	22	26	27	30
Josefsthal	—	—	—	—	—	2	Maxdorf	4	5	10	15	14	3	Josefsthal	9	—	8	9	8	12	Maxdorf	16	19	15	23	23	27
Maxdorf	—	1	2	1	1	2	Wiesenthal	2	1	4	2	4	2	Maxdorf	4	—	14	15	17	11	Wiesenthal	17	26	24	25	27	28
Wiesenthal	4	3	7	10	12	2	Neudorf	—	9	14	10	9	2	Wiesenthal	4	15	40	41	40	50	Neudorf	8	8	8	5	7	6
Neudorf	7	5	6	5	8	10	Kukan	2	1	9	5	9	4	Neudorf	10	4	7	11	8	4	Kukan	3	5	6	8	13	2
Kukan	30	23	32	35	38	48	Marschowitz	—	2	3	4	3	1	Kukan	1	—	3	7	7	8	Marschowitz	2	6	6	7	7	—
Marschowitz	4	1	1	—	—	1	Labau	—	—	—	—	1	—	Marschowitz	—	—	2	2	1	1	Labau	1	23	6	6	10	6
Labau	1	1	—	—	1	1	Dalleschitz	—	—	—	—	1	—	Labau	—	—	—	—	—	3	Dalleschitz	2	7	4	2	1	2
Dalleschitz	1	2	—	—	—	1	Buletschnei	—	1	—	—	—	—	Dalleschitz	—	—	—	1	1	3	Reichenau	—	1	5	7	8	8
Buletschnei	3	1	—	—	—	—	Reichenau	—	—	—	1	1	2	Buletschnei	—	—	1	2	1	1	Proschwitz	2	2	1	1	1	1
Reichenau	2	2	3	4	5	2	Radl	—	—	1	—	—	—	Reichenau	—	—	1	1	1	2	Morchenstern	45	38	30	35	38	61
Radl	—	—	—	1	2	2	Proschwitz	—	—	1	—	—	—	Morchenstern	5	—	29	27	35	48	Albrechtsdorf	24	50	61	61	59	56
Morchenstern	5	1	4	9	17	20	Morchenstern	19	11	33	50	50	13	Albrechtsdorf	—	6	7	11	12	4	Tannwald	4	7	3	4	5	5
Tannwald	1	1	3	5	10	7	Albrechtsdorf	2	2	9	5	9	7	Polaun	—	—	—	4	—	—	Schumburg	—	1	—	—	—	—
Schumburg	—	—	—	—	—	1	Tannwald	—	1	—	—	1	1	Tannwald	5	—	4	7	5	3	Prichowitz	7	7	7	9	10	10
Prichowitz	1	—	—	—	—	—	Prichowitz	4	1	1	3	—	2								Polaun	15	18	17	24	29	31
Polaun	—	1	—	—	—	—	Polaun	2	5	2	—	—	—														
Summa	142	141	153	190	219	276	Summa	80	91	161	173	155	94	Summa	43	22	134	171	169	174	Summa	196	268	238	275	293	314

Statistics about the expansion of the Gablonz industry between 1856 and 1876.

Bijouterie from Gablonz, circa 1840. Early bijouterie was dominated by glass elements. The three brooches on the left combine lampworked flowers; the two brooches on the right include large glass elements. The upper square is painted, and the lower circular element may be composed of mosaic or millefiori.

A brooch including a large millefiori element, made in the middle of the 19th century in Gablonz.

A lady wearing a large mosaic brooch, 1870s.

Beads, buttons, gemstones and bijouterie became the most important articles of the Gablonz industry besides *Kristallerie*, larger items that could be molded or cut including perfume bottles, toilette sets, writing sets, and paperweights. During the 18th and most of the 19th centuries, the Gablonzers provided foreign markets with elements — the gemstones, beads and some buttons — which were taken to distant capitals to be mounted in fashionable goods and accessories. Evening gowns and ball toilettes were lavishly decorated with blown beads from Morchenstern. Walking costumes and afternoon dresses were completed with cut and painted buttons from Wiesenthal. Hats were ornamented with glass flowers and fruit lampworked by cottage workers high up in the valleys of the Isermountains. Accessories like haircombs and belt buckles glittered with "Bohemian diamonds" from Seidenschwanz. And ever so glamorous, colorful handcut glass gemstones were mounted along with the "diamonds" into the fashionable jewelry manufactured in cities like Paris and London.

By the early 19th century, the demand from fashionable markets had already reached such a high level that in the 1820s Gablonz makers exported about 2.4 billion cut beads a year.[1] Some quick-thinking merchants realized that they could earn much greater profits from selling finished jewelry, not just the "raw material," the elements. Beginning in the 1830s, a growing number of Gablonz craftsmen began making lines of fashion jewelry, including ear-pendants hung with elaborate glass drops, and large rectangular *Biedermeier* brooches with sizable elements of ornamented glass. The industry grew from just glass-making and glass refinery to encompass jewelry production as well, though of course glasswork was featured prominently in the early Gablonz jewelry. It would not be unjust to say that the Gablonz jewelers' metalwork served merely to frame spectacular pieces of glass art.

The metalworking craftsmen — the *Gürtler*— who composed such jewelry had in fact been creating jewelry since the 18th century, though in those early periods they had limited their production to the creation of traditional costume jewelry. Only in this new phase, due to the initiative of the merchants and businessmen, did they start to aim at a wider market.

By 1860, the concentration of capable craftsmen and the quality of their products were great enough to attract various important trading companies from German capitals to this little "marketplace" far away in the mountains. (Gablonz was officially registered as a marketplace; only in 1866 did it officially become a town.) In the late 1880s, the Gablonz jewelry makers transformed 8000 tons of glass and 400 tons of metal into jewelry and adornments. Ninety-five percent of this was exported to foreign markets, while only 5% was kept for distribution within the boundaries of the Habsburg monarchy.[2]

Three main factors maintained Gablonz makers and exporters as crucial members of the world jewelry community. First, they continued to supply the glass elements — stones and beads — to be mounted and assembled elsewhere, as well as metal elements to be set and combined in foreign bijouterie industries. They also presented new collections of their own high-quality bijouterie each year, either according to their own characteristic designs or in close accordance with the prevailing fashion trends and artistic tendencies. These collections were bought by renowned retailers from all over the world and were sold (expensively) under the retailers' labels. Lastly, the Gablonzers covered every imaginable fashion accessory market, and sold goods that were within every consumer's range.

Once the important exporters settled in the area, Gablonz was fully equipped with skilled personnel for all phases of the jewelry-making and marketing industry. From that point on, the beads, buttons and bijouterie of this small Bohemian region were ready to conquer the world.

Necklace composed of lampworked flowers, from Gablonz in the early 20th century. Each flower is worked onto a metallic pin, which is then attached to a metal base. These flowers are made by means of the same fundamental process as those in the illustration of assorted bijouterie from 1840. This lampworking "in the Venetian style" can be documented in Gablonz beginning in the early 19th century.

Brooch from Gablonz composed of two flowers and a bird , circa 1880. This piece is typical of Gablonz bijouterie until the last third of the 19th century, assembled from patterned wire and incorporating natural themes and elements.

A lady wearing a brooch similar to the one at left; photograph from around 1890. The woman's dress is ornamented with faceted beads most likely produced in Gablonz.

Three buttons pressmolded with fancy patterns in high relief, from Gablonz in the late 19th century. Since the late 1860s, the making of such buttons was a leading branch of the industry. No other item presented such a challenge to imaginative design.

Two bundles of gold-lined blown beads from Morchenstern, early 20th century. Gold lining was introduced by Iwan Weiskopf in 1898, allowing Morchenstern makers to hold a virtual monopoly on this type of bead until 1945.

A pressmolded stone, a silver brooch and a pendant, all with Art Nouveau motifs; from Gablonz at the turn of the century. The Gablonz makers always adapted their creations to the mercurial demands of fashion and to the ever-changing trends of the fine art world.

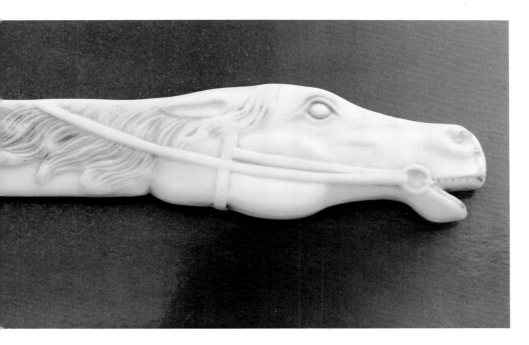

Celluloid handle simulating ivory, from turn-of-the-century Gablonz. Celluloid began to be used by Gablonzers in the late 1870s.

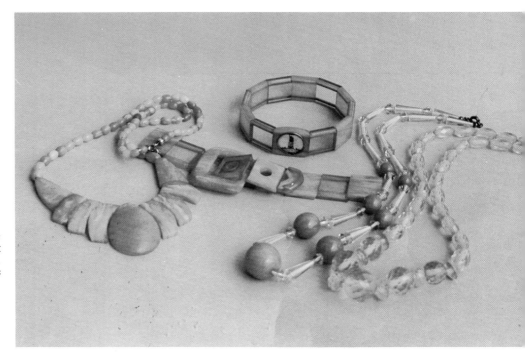

Necklaces and bracelets made in Gablonz from various amber-colored synthetic materials, first third of the 20th century. In the early 1900s, Gablonz became a leading center for plastic bead production.

An enameled brooch set with a satin glass cabochon from Gablonz, early 20th century. Satin glass has been one of the most admired varieties of bijouterie glass since the 19th century. In the 1890s, Gablonz artisans began to use this enamelling technique on a larger scale.

Two pendants composed in elaborate Gürtler-work, from Gablonz, 1930s. The gilded elements are partially enameled, set with topaz-colored glass stones and glass marcasites.

A Gablonz bracelet composed of coral-colored pressmolded stones, 1920s or 1930s. In the background is molded glass from the "Ingrid" collection by Henri Schlevogt of Gablonz, 1930s. High relief pressmolded designs like this were inspired by the 19th century buttonwork of the bijouterie industry. In the 1920s, this type of glass became especially fashionable; it was no longer molded in just the traditional black and opalescent shades, but in stone glasses like "malachite," "lapis lazuli," "carnelian" or "coral." This design line has been copied very successfully by Japanese manufacturers since the 1930s.

Filigree brooch set with amethyst-colored stones, Gablonz, 1920s/1930s. This brooch, which at first glance appears to be a rather standard piece, was painstakingly composed with the time-consuming methods of wire construction. It represents one important variety of genuine filigree work as it was made by the Gürtler in Gablonz.

A silvered clip composed of stamped filigree elements, set with stones, from Gablonz, 1920s/1930s. This type of filigree work was introduced in the second half of the 19th century.

Pressmolded glass clasp, from Gablonz, 1920s/1930s. Items like this, with strong colors and metallic coatings, represented a very important line of design for the Gablonz bijouterie.

Elements for chandeliers, Gablonz, turn of the century. Pendants like these were standard production beginning in the mid-18th century.

Various items in glass colored with uranium, from Gablonz, 19th and 20th centuries. The use of uranium for coloring glass was first recommended by the chemist Klaproth, in the late 18th century. The Riedels were among the first to produce it on a large scale, and it became one of the most successful types of glass of Bohemian origin.

Three pieces of jewelry with chrome-aventurine stones. The stones were produced in Gablonz, 19th and early 20th century; the mounts are of various origins. The Riedel glassworks were great pioneers in producing new colored glasses, and the glassmaker Johann Bengler, at the Klein-Iser glassworks, was an important factor in this. In 1879, Klein-Iser began to offer a variety of copper-aventurine as well.

The Glassworks

The Gablonz area had a remarkable glass-making tradition. Nearly a dozen glasshouses were founded within the second half of the 16th century, almost exclusively by members of three important dynasties, the Schürer, the Wander and the Preussler. However, none of these renowned glassworks survived the first half of the 18th century. Many factors contributed to this decline. Most significantly, however, the glass masters of those dynasties held too strongly to old traditions, and were unable to respond to the challenges of the new era, mass production and ever-expanding markets.

The Riedel Family

The disappearance of the old glasshouses was closely followed by a new beginning. This renewal, which developed into the most prosperous period of glass-making in Gablonz, is closely linked to the name Riedel. In the early 1750s, Johann Leopold Riedel (1726-1800) became the tenant of the Antoniwald glasshouse. Riedel was a descendant of one of the region's legendary glass merchants, a businessman responsible for opening up new overseas and European markets for Gablonz glass. Continuing in the family field Johann Leopold Riedel offered the usual Bohemian glasshouse products: drinking glasses, all kinds of bottles and many other utilitarian glassware. In addition, he offered various types of pendants for chandeliers, and small bottles (1.5 to 6 inches in height) meant to be used as scent bottles, tobacco flasks and perfume bottles. These little molded bottles were soon to become the greatest commercial success of the area. Excavations at the site of the Karlshütte glasshouse, which operated from 1758 to 1775, revealed that the choice of colors offered by Riedel in those early years was already considerable, including crystal, milk-white, opaline, light blue, dark blue, green, rose and opaque red.

Advertisement for perfume, Germany, late 1920s. The Gablonz area provided Europe and North America with perfume bottles of every type and in a wide range of qualites.

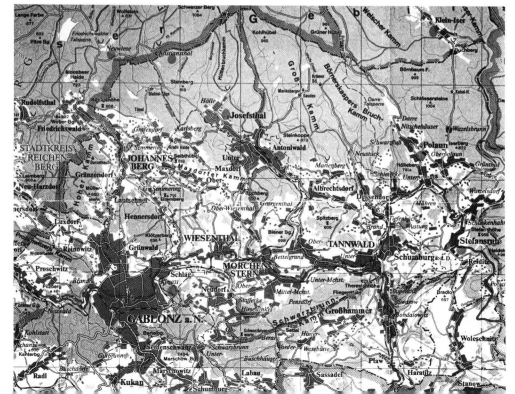

Map of the area, indicating the various glassworks of the Riedel clan.

Glass canes in various sizes, of modern production. The smaller canes are used for freeehand lampworking, while the larger ones are the standard size for molding tong production.

Soon, Johann Leopold was able to lease additional glassworks to meet the increasing demand for Riedel-glass. His glass was so popular in North Bohemia that the merchants and the glass-makers of the Gablonz area took him to court in 1766. Riedel was accused of not supplying them sufficiently, favoring his better-renowned clients in the Haida-Steinschönau area instead.

No matter how successful his business grew, however, Johann Leopold Riedel was the bondsman of the local nobility, just like everyone else living and working on the grounds of the Bohemian upper class. He was completely dependent on their goodwill, and his business was struck a powerful blow when they discovered a better-paying use for their timber than the fueling of glassworks. They started to disapprove of the "destructive use" of their forests by glass-makers, and in 1774 decided not to renew their contracts with Riedel.

Such subservience and forced dependence threatened all of Riedel's entrepreneurial activities, so he set out to gain full civil rights for himself. He succeeded. Armed with his "letter of release," dated February 28, 1776, he founded Christiansthal, the first of his self-owned glassworks.

In the following Riedel generation, Johann Leopold's eldest son Anton Leopold (1762-1821) proved to be a most successful businessman. He managed not only to satisfy his customers in Haida and Steinschönau, but also to reconcile the makers and merchants of Gablonz. The records of Neuwiese, another Riedel glassworks, show that since at least 1790 its production was well-adjusted to the needs of the Gablonz industry, which in the second half of the 18th century had just started to develop its specialized features. The glassworks still focused on producing crystal, but this crystal was then worked into small items such as bottles and pendants, which were then given to independent refiners in the valleys of the Isermountains or in small villages like Gablonz for further decoration. Besides these crystal items and some articles of colored glass, the Riedel glassworks supplied canes and tubes for lampworkers. It is also recorded that since at least 1803 they delivered the stronger canes for pressmolding workshops.

The Riedels tried twice in vain to get the honor "*staatlich privilegierte Glasfabrik*" ("Privileged Glass Factory") for their glassworks. The quality of their products was without a doubt up to the necessary standards. Therefore, the denial was most likely caused by the owners of other important glassworks, noblemen who did not appreciate seeing the "bourgeois" Riedel honored at their level.

The generation of Anton Leopold conducted the family business through the difficult years of Napoleon's imperialism, during which the European economy was destroyed. The next Riedel generation saw a European economic expansion, though, and they profited greatly from it. This generation was represented by two strong leaders, Karl Josef and Franz Anton, each of whom split off into a separate branch — the Reinowitz branch and the Polaun branch, respectively.

The Reinowitz branch of the Riedel Dynasty

Karl Josef Riedel (1803-1875) — son of Johan Leopold's younger son — developed Christiansthal into one of the most advanced glassworks of the area. It had two galleries for drawing canes, and thus was well-adapted to the special needs of the bijouterie industry. In 1875, the *glasshütte* converted to the most modern type of coal-firing. The exceptional expansion of this industry allowed Karl-Josef to regain the lease for the Zenker glassworks in Antoniwald, where his grandfather had started the dynasty. In 1868 he had also been able to buy a glasshouse in Hinter-Josefsthal which had been founded in 1864 by the glass-merchant Andreas Jantsch from Wiesenthal. Jantsch, like many other glass-merchants, felt the urge to enlarge the glass-making capacity of Gablonz as greatly as the overwhelming demand for their products would allow.

In 1838, Karl-Josef Riedel had inherited one glasshouse with a single furnace; when he died in 1875 he left to his three sons three Riedel plants with a total of five furnaces. Within the next 70 years this branch expanded to include six glassworks:

—The modern Kamnitz glassworks, which was erected in 1910 in a location especially well-suited to the needs of the glass-cutters in the Kamnitz valley. It replaced the Zenkner glassworks. They pressmolded such articles as perfume bottles, salt cellars, ink bottles, pendants and optical lenses.
—The Josefsthal glassworks, which was modernized and equipped with a 200 m. gallery for drawing canes to supply the bijouterie industry. The bangle boom which began in the 1870s caused further specialization in this production, and the glassworks alone is said to have had a daily output of 2000 bangles.
—The Unter-Maxdorf glassworks, a modern facility opened in 1904 because Josefsthal could not supply enough canes to satisfy the market. At Unter-Maxdorf, they produced nothing but canes.
—Two Reinowitz glassworks. In 1882, Leopold Riedel (1846-1926),the younger son of Karl Josef, had already opened a modern glassworks in Reinowitz. The family's glassworks in Christiansthal—originally chosen because the surrounding forests were still available for glass-making purposes—proved in the long run to be at a distinct disadvantage because of its isolated location. Thus, the family chose not to rebuild it after it burned down in 1887, instead deciding to build a second plant in Reinowitz a year later. In Reinowitz, they produced mainly crystal and black glass, continuing the production of bangles which had begun in Christiansthal in the 1860s.
—Another Reinowitz glasshouse. Karl Riedel, Jr. (1897-1945), the grandson of Leopold, introduced new methods of glass-press- ing in 1926. His financial success with this process allowed him to acquire this third Reinowitz glass house in 1927.

After the expulsion of the German craftsmen from Gablonz, the last Reinowitz Riedel, Leopold (b. 1901), became the director of the main laboratory of the Gerresheimer glassworks in Düsseldorf in 1949.

The Polaunbranch
of the Riedel dynasty

The other important branch of the Riedel family included Franz Anton Riedel (1786-1844), who had combined a strong business sense with great aesthetic talents, creating and producing some of the most beautiful designs in the company's history. Like his father, he had tried to incorporate a glass refinery into the glassworks, and like his father he failed. He was unable to compete with the growing number of independent refinery workshops, and had to accept the new interdependent structure for glass-making which the glass merchants had imposed. Franz Anton's efforts were the last initiative in Gablonz to re-establish a "traditional" glasshouse, in which all steps of glass-making and glass decoration were executed under one roof.

Franz Anton played an important role in the introduction of uranium-colored glass to the Gablonz glass-making industry. Indeed, the two main shades of this glass were named after his daughters, "Anna" yellow and "Eleonoren" green. He was probably also the main force behind the decision to produce colored composition in the Zenker glassworks in Antoniwald.

The first Riedel glasshouse in Polaun.

Eduard Enzmann   Polaun — alte Riedel-Hütte (Federzeichnung)

Perfume bottle and covered box, by Josef Riedel, Polaun, 1930s. Glass in such modern designs was made by Riedel for a major exporter, Gebrüder Feix, in Albrechtsdorf. It was meant primarily for the German market, since the British and American markets generally preferred more traditional pieces.

The recorded recipes[1] give us a unique insight into the choice of colors available as early as the 1830s in Gablonz. The colors offered by the Zenker glassworks were most likely no more than a basic selection; large composition-makers offered much more extensive listings—composition-maker Franz Zenkner offered no less than for shades of red during those years. The recipes reveal how an alert businessman had gained for his company a proper share of a promising production line market, which until that time had been held exclusively by the composition-makers.

Between 1830 and 1840, Franz Anton's nephew Josef Riedel (1816-1894), soon to become the legendary "glass king of the Iser Mountains," was introduced by his uncle to the business and the secrets of glass-making in the Zenker glassworks. In 1840 he married his cousin Anna Riedel, and in 1844 they inherited the Zenker and the Klein-Iser glassworks, founded in 1828. Josef did more than just preserve and continue to extend the heritage: he represented the transition to modern glass manufacturing.

In 1849, he bought a glassworks in Polaun which had been founded in 1846 by the successful glass merchant Ignaz Friedrich. Like many other glass merchants who began manufacturing to maintain an adequate glass supply, Friedrich was more than ready to withdraw from the job as soon as a glass-making expert was ready to take over. Polaun was well-situated near the most important road, so Josef Riedel transferred his main office there. In the decades that followed, he created a Riedel imperium in Polaun, employing 1250 workers in three cane glassworks, a bead factory, two glass refineries, a bronze foundry, a cotton mill and a cotton manufacturing plant. Additionally, in 1878 he founded a glass factory in Untermaxdorf from which he supplied the glass-cutters in the Kamnitz valley with pressed bottles and other similar articles. In this plant he also responded to the needs of the bangle industry.

In 1879 Josef Riedel bought another glassworks, this one in Neudorf. It had been founded by Ignaz Kleinert, one of the self-made men so typical of Gablonz. He had started as a poor cottage worker and bead-cutter, but died as a rich manufacturer of glass, beads and buttons.

Ink set, by Josef Riedel, Polaun, 1930s. The attractive satin glass was used mainly for beads, buttons and gemstones, but it also lent itself well to larger items like this. *(Courtesy of the Museum Warmensteinach)*

In the two successive generations of Riedels, the Polaun branch expanded even further. Between 1899 and 1912 they founded six more glassworks, one exclusively for blowing glass. In 1915 they took over the Schicketanz glassworks, where they continued to produce canes and tubes of the highest quality.

As the Reinowitz branch did, the Polaun Riedels counted among their younger members (those born in the second half of the 19th century) various glass technologists. These innovators made sure to implement the most advanced scientific methods in their factories.

The chemist Josef Riedel, Jr. (1862-1924) applied the study of colloids to glass production. This was of central importance for glass-making because colloids are crucial to glass-coloring.* His son, the engineer Walter Riedel (1895-1974), took a major part in producing advanced technical glass, including large picture tubes used for air space monitoring by the German air force. After the war, Arno Riedel (1897-1964) was withheld by the Czech until 1950, while Walter Riedel was taken to Russia to supervise a glass laboratory for ten years.

The confiscation of the Riedel properties in 1945 brought the end of an era, but not the end of a most creative glass dynasty. After his release, Arno cooperated in reconstructing the bijouterie industry in Neugablonz, while Walter and his son Claus took over an abandoned glassworks in Kufstein/Austria in 1957. Walter and Claus's new venture was to become the world-famous company Riedel-Glas Austria.

The Riedels are unique in the history of glass-making. They maintained a reputation as suppliers of the world's finest glass and glassware for an uninterrupted sequence of ten generations. Each generation not only preserved the heritage of their forefathers, but reacted in an ever-new and creative way to the challenges of a growing, changing market.

***

* Colloids are clouds of miniscule particles suspended in the glass, which make us perceive specific colors.

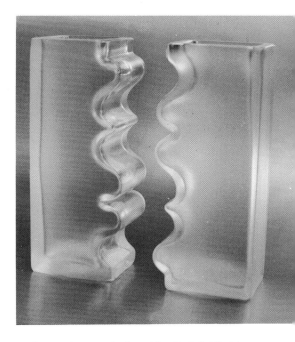

Segmentvasen, designed by Carl J. Riedel, 1967, at the Riedel-Glas Austria company. This piece was awarded the "Premio Internazionale Vincenza" in 1972. "In a period which abhorred ornament, Riedel designed vases with the mathematical sine motif of reciprocal curves. The designer was prompted by the idea of creating decorative glass vessels which could be used as vases or as purely ornamental glass objects." (Riedel, 1991, p. 132)

Part of a belt buckle, transformed into a brooch. It is made from silver filigree set with artificial gemstones. Traditional "costume jewelry" from Northern Germany, mid 19th century. Northern Germany in particular acquired their stones from Gablonz because of the River Elbe provided direct transportation between the two areas.

Two "fire-gilded" clasps including composition stones, circa 1830. The metalwork was done in Germany, while the stones were manufactured in Gablonz.

A selection of artificial gemstones in traditional colors, including "amethyst" and "topaz." Neugablonz, 1960s. The glass was composed by the Scheibler glassworks, and handcut by Anton Brückner, both descendants from families involved in Gablonz glassmaking since the 17th century.

Composition Makers

The glass for artificial stones and for some kinds of beads was much different from the glass used by glass-blowers. One distinguishing characteristic was its unusual composition; it was generally rich in lead, for example. Up to the 17th century, this glass was composed for the bijouterie industry almost exclusively by the Muranese glass-makers.

In Northern Europe, the making of such glass was cultivated on a rather hidden, small level, among the alchemists. The secrets of this type of composition were finally spread by the publication of *De Arte Vitraria*, a collection of glass "recipes," in 1611. Compiled by the Italian Antonio Neri, the book was soon translated into many languages, and became the most important glass-making manual for European craftsmen. While there had been other Northern European compilations of glassmaking recipes, none had make a great impact on the general practice of the craft. One of these was the *Kunstbuch*, the "art book" of Behringer von Kotzau, written between 1562 and 1574. Since it was handwritten, however, it never had great circulation, and its recipes remained widely unknown.

The Gablonzers made many individual attempts to learn whatever secrets of Murano glass remained unpublished. The traditions and techniques of cutting natural gemstones (like the famous Bohemian garnet) were deeply rooted in the Bohemian town of Turnov a few kilometers south of Gablonz, but the region's business had suffered from the competition of much cheaper (artificial) stones from Murano and Venice. It is said that in the early 18th century, two Bohemians from Turnov — Wenzel and Franz Fischer — had worked in Murano to acquire the skills and transmit them to their native town.

The vigorous competition between Murano and Bohemia engendered stories of many such "spies," valiant glass-makers from both sides working secretly amidst the "enemy" to discover the foreign techniques and save their own region's business. One such story is of the Italian Giuseppe Briatti, who is said to have learned through his 18th century espionage the secrets of making brilliant Bohemian crystal—however, research by renowned glass historian Silvano Tagliapietra disclosed in 1991 that there is very little truth to this account, which has been spread only too willingly by less scrutinizing scholars. Still, no matter how suspect the details of these "spy stories" are, there remains one indisputable fact: both the Muranese and the Bohemians tried during this era to appropriate and adapt the inside tricks of their strongest competitors in order to enhance (or at least maintain) their competitive edge in European and overseas markets.

In 1774, Minister of State Count Zinsendorf reported from Turnov that "there are 110 craftsmen living here who reproduce artificial gemstones and strass [glass stones]."[1] Further records clearly indicate that composition-making and cutting began to concentrate in the Gablonz area in at least the 1780s. The craftsmen in Gablonz and in the surrounding valleys were well-versed in the techniques of glass-making and cutting; moreover, they had waterdriven wheels at their disposal, simplifying the extremely labor-intensive cutting work. A great increase in the number of significant composition-makers in Gablonz was recorded after the late 18th century as this profession grew rapidly in importance.

Bernhard Unger started a composition workshop in Gablonz in the 1780s. He and his brother Anton had been successful exporters of

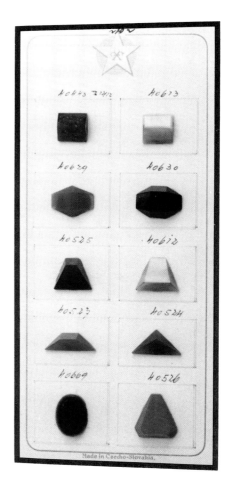

Sample card of pressmolded stones from Fried Fréres, Gablonz, late 1920s. A selection of composition stones in such traditional colors as "onyx," "lapis," "jade," "coral," and "carnelian."

Beads and necklaces made from coral composition, Gablonz, early 20th century through the 1930s. "Coral" was always a well-appreciated color among the beadmakers.

Red Composition

Special mention was often made of composition makers who worked in various shades of red. The shades' names are frequently listed in great detail separately from other colors, which may be referred to merely as "in many colors." This special attention to the varieties of red is the result of the enormous difficulty of achieving fine red shades. Thus red composition (and red glass in general) commanded very high prices, and red stones and beads were very much in demand.

Karl Josef and Franz Zenkner, as mentioned in this chapter, were renowned for their varieties of red glass. However, composition-maker Anton Mai, Sr., working between 1817 and 1820, is said to have produced the finest garnet-colored and ruby-colored composition for beads.[4]

artificial gemstones and later of buttons, but ventured into composition-making because they anticipated that an immense jewelry market for this glass would soon open up. The area's glassworks had not realized the potential of this burgeoning bijouterie industry, and were not producing as much glass as the Unger exporters knew would be needed. Bernhard Unger went so far as to start a glassworks of his own in Tiefenbach in 1786. In 1814 the brothers sold this thriving business to Franz and Anton Brückner, composition-makers in Antoniwald[2], allowing the Ungers to concentrate once again on their original calling. Thereafter, the Unger exporting business continued to be recorded as an important glass and bijouterie trading company.

During the early years of the 19th century, artificial gemstones became of central importance throughout Europe. The French "société pour l'encouragement de l'industrie" invited French makers to create artificial gemstones and strass "that could compete with German products." There can be little doubt that the German products to which the Frenchmen referred were largely products from Gablonz.

In 1810, in this atmosphere so conducive to high quality and profitability, the name Scheibler appeared for the first time on the list of composition-makers. The Scheiblers, notable for their exceptional turquoise and sapphire composition, became the finest composition-makers in Gablonz through the 19th century and until 1945, the time of the Sudetengermans' expulsion. They illustrate the remarkable continuity of craft that can be found among the leading Gablonz families.

In 1835 can be found one Anton Scheibler in Gablonz at #340, a Josef Scheibler at #243, and yet another Josef Scheibler at #259 — all successful composition-makers! (Numbers refer to site numbers, at that time usually used as a building's address.) Confusion over family names, obviously, was a problem in Gablonz. It became customary for Gablonzers to call one another not only by their Christian names, but also by a prefix referring either to a person's profession or to his address. In the 20th century the Scheiblers are registered in and around Gablonz in various professions, but they held primarily to their traditional family craft of glass-making. Thus, a hundred years after the aforementioned jumble of names and addresses, the Scheiblers were still thickly scattered across the area: Anton Scheibler, a composition-maker, lived in Mühlgasse 33; Ernst Scheibler, another composition-maker, lived in Glasgasse 53; and Franz, yet another composition-maker, lived in Hubertusgasse 2.[3]

Another important composition-making family at this time was the Zenkner clan. Karl Josef Zenkner combined the production and the marketing of composition in his dealings. He was one of Gablonz's most successful representatives at the 1829 exhibition of Bohemian glass in Prague, and was widely known for his beautiful carnelian glass. Franz Zenkner, a widely respected composition-maker for many decades, was known for his tubes in a great variety of reds, including gold-ruby, copper-ruby and rose.

J.W. Jäckel filed for a patent in 1835 for his "Venetianer Fluss," as aventurine was called at that time. Another reputable composition-maker, Coelestin Wagner from Wiesenthal, was known for his "Mosaikglas auf Venetianer Art," which may have been millefiori glass. Wagner and Jäckel, both with their "Venetianer" glasses, make it quite clear whom the Gablonzers considered their main competitors for the important European and overseas markets.

In the 1830s and 1840s, the Gablonz area hosted about two dozen independent composition-makers; by 1860, 106 makers are listed. Paradoxically, however, by the last third of the 19th century the growth of Gablonz's glass market had resulted in a *reduction* of the number of listed composition-makers, and in 1873 only 67 composition-makers were listed. The enormous explosion of the industry in the 19th century required a constant supply of tubes and canes so large it could not be fulfilled by glassworks "en miniature" like those the composition-makers

A selection of necklaces with beads of two standard composition varieties, topaz-colored crystal and amber-colored satin glass. From Gablonz, 1920s and 1930s.

operated. Many craftsmen or workshops listed as composition-makers had expanded their businesses into full glassworks, taking their names off the "composition-maker" roster. Moreover, there was less demand for the specialized color-production services of the few composition-makers still listed, as a constantly increasing number of colors became standard at large glassworks. Hardly more than a dozen composition-makers remained in operation in 1897; this number was more or less constant until the 1930s.[5]

The Schicketanz family of Albrechtsdorf is typical of these composition-makers who transformed their interests into full glassworks. The clan had been raising composition-makers for generations, but in the early 20th century the brothers Robert and Ernst each began a separate glassworks.

Robert was a competent glass technologist who had worked in varous important glassworks throughout Europe before leasing a composition-workshop in Gablonz in 1903. In 1907 he took over the significant "Franz Breit & Sohn" glassworks in Schatzlar, and in 1911 he opened a new glassworks in Gablonz. With nine furnaces and 64 pots he supplied the bijouterie industry with exceptional colored glass and composition. Unfortunately, the company was not financially stable enough to survive the economic troubles of World War I, and folded.

Ernst Schicketanz did not expand his composition workshop in Albrechtsdorf into a proper glassworks until 1919, after World War I was over. Once established, he began to produce canes and tubes in standard colors. For some years he collaborated with Konrad Dressler, Sr. and his son Konrad, Jr., both members of a Gablonz dynasty that had begun in the 17th century. The Dresslers opened their own glassworks in Morchenstern in 1929, producing outstanding colored glass and composition. Their colors bore such traditional names as "Chrysopras" and "Carneol," revealing the company's strong link to early composition recipes which tried to imitate real gemstones. It would appear that the Dressler company is the last remnant of the Schicketanz legacy and tradition; in 1948, after World War II, descendants of the Dressler family founded the Kittel-glassworks in Neugablonz, becoming once again a major supplier of fine glass for bijouterie.

Despite such shuffling, composition-makers did not completely vanish from Gablonz's industry. To them was always left the most creative task of composing new specialty glasses, and of remaining the pioneers of fancy glass production. From the beginning of the 18th century to the middle of the 20th century, composition-makers consistently offered the greatest selection and the finest varieties of colored glass for bijouterie. However humble their workshops were, in the field of colored glass they were always ahead of even the largest and most important glassworks.

Various strands of beads, including gold- and silver-lined beads, Morchenstern, first third of the 20th century. Such lining was introduced in the 19th century by the Weiskopfs.

Glass Technology

In the Gablonz area during the 19th century, fine glass-making remained largely in the hands of "uneducated" glass masters, whose success was based upon empirical knowledge transmitted within families from generation to generation. But even in this remote region, production based on scientific methods took its place beside tradition in the second half of the 19th century.

Evidence of glass technology can be found not only in the large major glassworks, but also in smaller companies like the "Chemische Fabrik Morchenstern," founded in 1875 by Paul Weiskopf (1845-1879). Paul was the son of Hartwig Weiskopf (1810-1875), a forward-thinking doctor and a strong proponent of the water treatments introduced by the German doctor Kneipp — treatments which in those years were still vehemently rejected by the medical establishment.

Dr. Weiskopf's concern about the health of the poor brought him into close contact with glass-making. In this era, Bohemian beads were lined with a solution containing quicksilver (mercury) and lead, both toxic. As the workers sucked the liquid into the beads, they were gradually poisoned by the noxious fumes. In 1853, however, Dr. Weiskopf introduced the lining of glass beads with a silver solution, saving thousands of cottage workers from painful deaths.

Beginning in the 1860s, the competent articles of Paul Weiskopf, a chemist, began appearing in German journals. He was the first Gablonzer to spread through publication any of the region's highly concentrated glass-making knowledge. However skilled the Gablonz craftsmen were, they had not yet grown accustomed to documenting their immense knowledge or protecting it with patents. Thus they lost most of their priority rights to foreign makers during the second half of the 19th century. Paul Weiskopf touched upon this delicate problem in one of his first articles[1] when he referred to the fact that milk-white glass had long since been colored in Bohemian and Silesian glassworks with the constituent Kryolith. The procedure was later patented in the United States and became one of the most important techniques in commercial glass-making.

The story of another important article by Paul Weiskopf illustrates that even the publication of a procedure did not prevent illegitimate or fraudulent claims. In 1856, a Hungarian chemist had introduced the surface decoration of iridescence; such glass was shown for the first time at the World Fair in Vienna in 1873. Paul Weiskopf was extremely fascinated by this glass, but because the original maker was very secretive about his procedure Weiskopf had to experiment extensively to find his own method, which he published in 1876. After the World Fair in Paris in 1878, iridized glass became a craze in Europe and North America. One new patent followed another, though none of the procedures protected by these new patents included any detail not described in the text of Paul Weiskopf!

During his short life, Paul Weiskopf researched and developed the most varied fields of glass-making. Living in such a fertile glass-making area, he was able to combine theory and practice in a unique way. His research and work was strongly rooted in the practical glass-making knowledge that virtually saturated the Gablonz air. Weiskopf simply condensed the available knowledge, submitted the empirical procedures to scientific testing and described his results in proper scientific detail.

Advertisement for the "Chemische Fabrik Morchenstern" company, 1880.

In this way, Weiskopf also made important contributions to the field of "stone" glass. Such opaque glass can be achieved in a great many ways. The most attractive varieties show only a delicately marbled structure, like that found in real marble or on chalcedonies. The best-known varietiy of stone-glass is certainly the Muranese "calcedonio," which has been produced for centuries. In the early 19th century, Bohemian varieties such as the red "Hyalith" produced by Count Buquoy's Georgenthal glassworks became comparably famous, as did the various stone-glasses of Josef Zich and the so-called Lythialin glasses created by Friedrich Egermann. In the 1880s the stone-glasses of the manufacturer Lötz (Loetz), named "Karneol" and "Malachit," became quite renowned as well. These famous makers make it easy to forget that high-quality stone-glasses had been produced almost anonymously throughout the 19th century by Gablonz makers for use in beads, buttons and gemstones.

Paul Weiskopf had been attentive to this kind of glass since at least the 1860s. The Weiskopf company had even filed a patent for a type of stone-glass with a surface treatment like that of the famous Egermann glasses, which accentuate gradations within the glass. Paul Weiskopf referred on repeated occasions to the successful use of such glass by the makers of beads, buttons and gemstones.

Weiskopf also noted the difficulties with which glass-blowers had to cope when working with this type of glass. According to him, only the manufacturer Josef Riedel in Polaun produced satisfactory quality in blown stone-glass. At the World Fair in Vienna in 1873, Riedel had shown items of stone-glass in brown tinges which Weiskopf considered comparable in quality to the gray-green "calcedonio" from Murano, which also got considerable exposure at that Fair.[2]

The work of Paul Weiskopf was not limited to art glass; he experimented in the field of technical glass as well. When textiles made from spun glass became a craze in the 1870s, Paul Weiskopf used the same threads for a more pragmatic purpose. He manufactured new filters for industrial use out of glass fibers to replace the customry filters made from, of all things, asbestos! Thus, the Weiskopf family made yet another contribution in the interest of the health of the workers.[3]

After Paul Weiskopf's sudden death, his brother Iwan (1848-1911) took over the company. Like his father, he was a doctor, and he was similarly concerned about the wellfare of the workers. One of his most important achievments to their benefit was the foundation of the "Cooperation of the lampworkers for blown beads" (*Produktivgenossenschaft der Hohlperlenerzeuger*) in 1898. He continued to work in the field of lining beads, and shortly before the turn of the century introduced the method of lining them with real gold.

A beaker molded from stoneglass and a paperweight made of marble. The beaker is probably from Gablonz, late 19th/early 20th century.

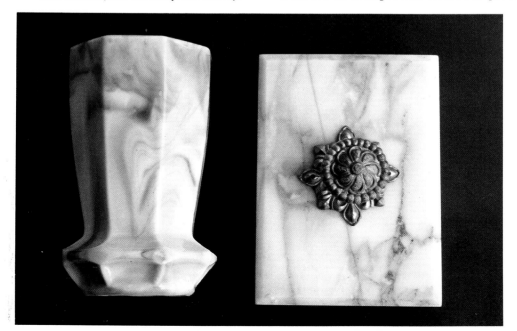

Cutting & Engraving

...this report is not complete without a reference to the cutting workshops. They are found in all sizes ranging from the humble and low-built rooms which include one or two wheels in addition to the few pieces of personal furniture, up to the large halls which include dozens of wheels. As manifold as the workshops are the tasks. Men, women boys and girls bend over the turning wheels and press beads, buttons, bottles and vases against them. The sharp sound produced by such work hardly impedes the lively chatting of the workers....(Leutelt, 1932)

In 1715, the guild of stonecutters in Turnau had secured for themselves the exclusive right of cutting composition, but the limited capacities of the hand-driven cutting devices they used finally induced them to compromise with the Gablonz glass-cutters. The "glass artist," as the glass-cutters were called, founded their own guild in Gablonz in 1737. They worked on water-driven wheels or, in the small cottage shops, on hand- and foot-driven wheels. In 1764 the two guilds concluded an agreement in Seidenschwanz which allowed the stonecutters to use the glass-cutters' cutting devices, while the latter got the right to cut composition. This tradition of extremely strict regulation was a major factor in the eventual dissolution of the European guilds, but of course there were many attempts to work around the regulations. By 1757, a certain Wenzel Hübner (1702-1790) had founded "The Guild of Glass-Stone-cutters" in Seidenschwanz. There can be little doubt that they cut composition too! Hübner, the most successful stone-merchant of the 18th century, employed up to 30 workers in his workshop.

The cutting of glass and stones became the most important work for refineries in Gablonz. By 1829, the area counted 152 cutting workshops employing 1865 cutters. An additional 1071 cottage workers lived in the Gablonz area, generally cutting small items like beads, stones and stoppers with hand and foot-driven wheels.

Advertisement for the stone exporter Ferdinand Schwarz, 1924.

A cutting workshop in the Gablonz area, 1913.

The "shearing" of stones. Pressmolded stones are first sheared, and then cut. Stones of this size are always hand-cut. *(Courtesy of Ernst Seidel, Warmensteinach)*

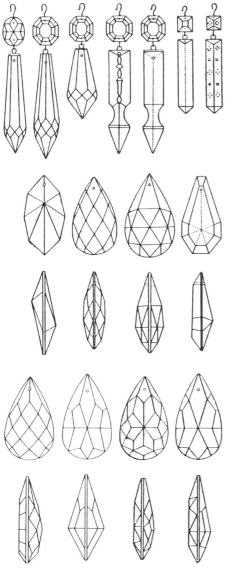

The cutting of *Kristallerie*, however, had to be done on water-driven wheels in the valleys, or in places like Josefsthal and Untermaxdorf. Because of this dependance on natural facilities, the production of these large articles remained located in valleys such as the Kamnitz- and the Dessevalley, in Josefsthal and Untermaxdorf. Each of these regions developed its own local glass-cutting characteristics, by means of which their products can be differentiated. The cutters in the upper Kamnitzvalley cut primarily on vertical wheels. This type of cutting was called "kugeln," because the vertical wheel produces (among other patterns) a convex print on the glass; *kugeln* derives from the word *kugel*, "globe." The cutters in the Dessevalley worked predominantly with horizontal rotating wheels, thus producing flat cuts, called an "English cut" (*Englisch-Schliff*).

The stonecutters moved during the 19th century from their original headquarters in Seidenschwanz and Morchenstern (southeast of Gablonz) to Reichenau and Radl (southwest of Gablonz). The finest and most sparkling finish of the cut stones was achieved on tin-wheels, and correspondingly the stones were called "tin stones." In the later 19th and early 20th centuries, the phrase "Tin Stones of Radl" (*Radler Zinnsteine*) assured buyers of the highest quality.

Standard cutting patterns on pendants. Similar patterns were applied to other items as well.

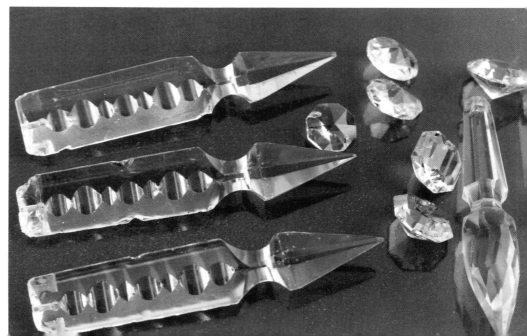

Originally, even the small stones of high quality were cut one by one. To allow the controlled cutting of the tiniest stones, they were cemented on top of a wooden peg (*Kittstock*). This was inserted into a simple device which allowed the craftsmen to tilt the stone at regular angles. The growing demand for simili-stones, as those artificial gemstones were called, and the strong competition of the stone industry in the French Juramountains forced the manufacturers in Gablonz to streamline their methods. To this end, they began to develop various cutting machines in the late 19th century.

A cut stone (7 cm), the masterpiece of Reinhold Feix (1873-1933). *(Courtesy of Mrs. Seidel, Warmensteinach)*

Hair ornament and necklace, Gablonz, late 19th/early 20th century. However simple the metalwork is on these mass-produced items, they include perfectly sparkling machine-cut stones.

Daniel Swarovski

One inventive manufacturer, Daniel Swarovski, was to become the world's best-known producer of machine-cut stones. Born in 1862 in Georgenthal to a glass-cutter father, Daniel nonetheless chose to learn the Gürtler craft. The family owned a small workshop where they produced hand-cut stones and riveted them onto accessory items such as brooches, haircombs and hatpins. These fashionable pieces were delivered mainly to the well-known exporter Feix. Feix was also the businessman who induced the Swarovskis to improve a machine for cutting buttons and who sent Daniel to visit the "First Electricity Exhibition" in Vienna in 1883.

This direct contact with modern technique was crucial for the inventive young man. In the following years he started a company together with Franz Weis. For the most part, they produced brooches and hatpins, which they marketed directly to Paris, without the intermediate

A little girl adorned with a diadem made of strass (artificial diamonds) on a fashionable postcard from 1911 Germany.

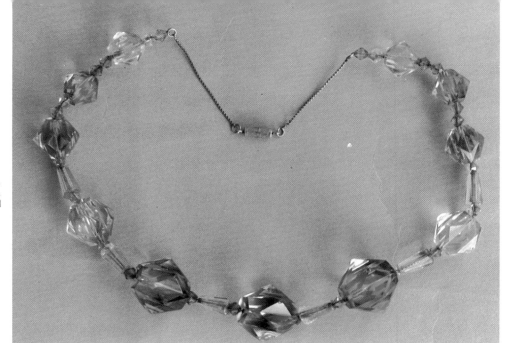

Necklace with cut beads from Gablonz, 1920s. Such beads were pressmolded, and then cut. Cutting of such intricacy was always executed by hand.

Another necklace with pressmolded and hand-cut beads from Gablonz, 1920s.

Brooch set mainly with machine-cut baguettes from Gablonz, early 20th century.

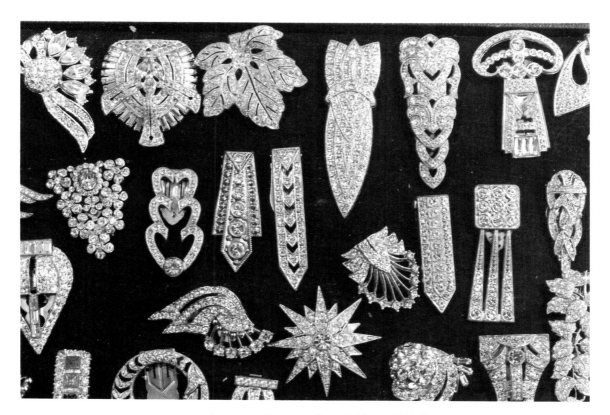

Clips set with strass from Gablonz, 1920s/
1930s. When these fashionable clips with inventive designs were mass-produced, the
stones were no longer handset into claw settings, but were instead merely glued to the
setting's base.

Clips and brooches set with strass, some from
the Gablonz area, 1920s/1930s.

Eduard Weis

of an exporter. Thus they overcame the anonymity imposed upon most of the makers and craftsmen in the Gablonz area, who never came in direct touch with their market and their clients. The business of the two young men expanded, and when they moved to new premises in Johannesthal near Reichenberg in 1886, they started production with about 70 employees.

Despite their success, a sudden change in fashion soon forced Swarovski and Weis to scale down the business. In 1889, Daniel Swarovski became technical advisor to one of the leading export houses, Gustav Strauss in Gablonz. He was given an experimental workshop in which he improved a new metal shank for buttons and improved the cutting and faceting of drawn beads. Enriched by the experience and experimentation, he returned to his own workshop in Johannesthal in 1891, and immediately started to improve his company's stonecutting methods. In 1892 he filed a patent for his first stonecutting device, and in 1893 he installed his first cutting machine.

In 1895, Swarovski and Weis's company moved to Wattens in Tyrol mainly because of the growing competition from other inventive makers in the closely-packed Gablonz area. Over the next decades in Wattens, the company grew into its role as a leading supplier of stones. Now, at the end of the 20th century, it counts more than 8,400 employees on its rosters!

The company not only excelled at improving the machinery but also at fine-tuning glass composition. One important advance in the 20th century was the development of identically shaded and colored stones, regardless of size. Before Swarovski's work, larger stones pressed from a particular glass composition would be more intense in shade than smaller stones of the same composition; the larger the gem, the stronger the color. This had not mattered in old-fashioned, widely spaced stone settings, but it became crucial in modern group settings such as channel setting, cluster setting and pavé setting, in which stones set nearly flush against one another allow for close color comparison.

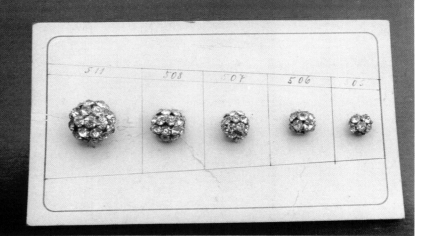

A sample card with strass beads from Gablonz, late 1920s. The sample card was assembled by exporter Rudolf Löwy of Gablonz, for his customer Bengel in Oberstein/Germany.

Handbag set with frosted cabochons and with strass from Gablonz, 1920s/1930s.

Two necklaces with prong-set strass from Gablonz, 1930s.

Necklace and bracelet set with strass and pressmolded "jade," signed KTF (Krussmann, Trifari, Fishel), 1935. Most of the important jewelry manufacturers in the United States got at least some of their stones from Gablonz or from Swarovski. Cohn & Rosenberger, later to become Coro, began in 1901 with a single small store on Broadway in New York; quickly becoming one of the leading jewelry manufacturers in the USA, they even had their own building in Gablonz.

Pendant and brooch by Ernst Seidel, Warmensteinach, 1980s. The pendant includes a large hand-cut stone.

A glass engraving by the famous Dominik Biemann, who received his training in the Harrach glassworks.

Engraving glass and metal

Within the intricate network of cooperating craftsmen, the metal engravers played a crucial role. Their craft had not been imported by foreign workers but had grown from local roots; engraving had been applied to glass from the start. In the Gablonz area, the engravers' most prosperous period occured during the second half of the 18th century and the first half of the 19th century. The most important engraving workshops were concentrated in Kukan. In the summertime, glass merchants from Kukan like Johann Kittel, Josef Kittel and August Ulbrich traveled with their engravers to fashionable spas in North Bohemia to sell their products. There, they could engrave the items immediately upon request, usually with the purchaser's family crest and initials or an inscription.

Towards the mid-19th century, the business slowed down considerably, partly because engraving was concentrating in the Haida-Steinschönau area, and partly because of changing fashions. Emmanuel Kittel (1812-1897), the son of Johann Kittel, was most likely the first one to respond to this situation. He realized the growing needs of the bijouterie industry for good molds, and around 1849 he started to do metal engraving. In the beginning, he used his glass-engraving tools for this new endeavor, but soon the metalworker Kajetan Schier in neighboring Dalleschitz provided him with appropriate tools, as well as with good metalworking advice. This early cooperation resulted in further fruitful contributions to the Gürtler profession. Schier constructed stamping and cutting tools, and Kittel became renowned for his excellent engravings on the glass-stamping tools. Other craftsmen from glass-making families also converted to metal engraving, including Leopold Kittel (1827-1864) and Johann Kittel (1840-1916).

A similar change occured in Morchenstern's industry as the glass-engraving market altered. Josef Seidel (1774-1840) had owned a prosperous cutting workshop and trading business, which had brought him into exhibitions as far away as Bremen. After Josef's death, the general glass-engraver's crisis affected his prosperous workshop too, and his sons were forced to close it. One son, Vinzenz Seidel (1803-1871), then began to specialize in engraving molds for buttons.

Eduard Weis (1835-1890) descended from another glass-engraving dynasty. In 1852 he became the mold-maker for the Riedel company in Antoniwald, and in 1858 settled in Wiesenthal to specialize in mold-engraving for buttons.

Still, good metal-engravers were always rare. In 1880, the area counted not more than twelve master engravers. Between the 1890s and the 1930s, their number remained fairly stable at 40.

Stone, hand-engraved with a heart, a cross and an anchor– the symbols of hope, faith and fidelity. Made in Gablonz in the late 19th century.

A button pressmolded with a deer and a dog, from Gablonz, 19th century. The animals are hand-gilded.

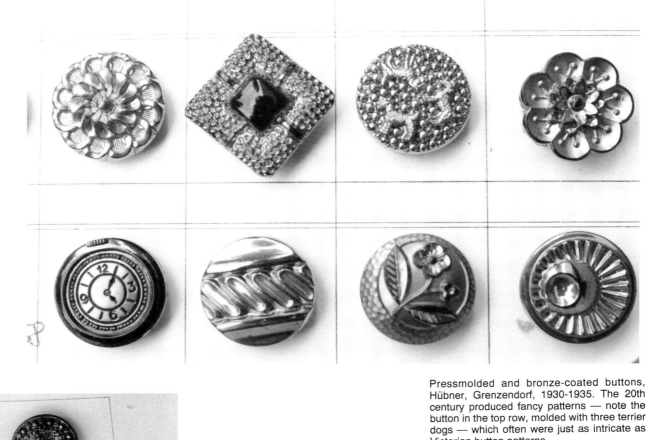

Pressmolded and bronze-coated buttons, Hübner, Grenzendorf, 1930-1935. The 20th century produced fancy patterns — note the button in the top row, molded with three terrier dogs — which often were just as intricate as Victorian button patterns.

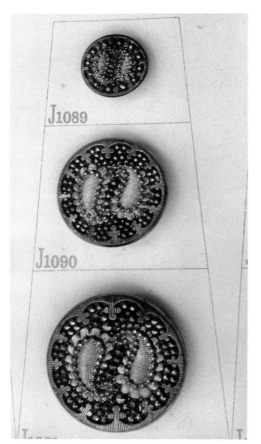

Pressmolded and gilded buttons from Gablonz, 1889/90. Intricate patterns were very popular in the last third of the 19th century, especially those that imitated other materials, including fabrics or metals like the marcasites of these buttons.

Two cameos. On the left, an early 20th century cameo on a (most likely) English mount. On the right, a 1960s cameo from Neugablonz. No motif required finer engraving talents than cameos did.

A pressmolding workshop in the Gablonz area, 1913. These buildings stood out from all the other humble houses around Gablonz, easily detectable because of their unusual roofs, which allowed the furnace heat and fumes to escape.

Pressmolding an Artificial Gem

To a spectator, the procedure for pressmolding artifical gemstones seems exceedingly simple; it it looks as if anyone could sit down and do it without any training. However, the craft is full of hidden intricacies.

The glass must be heated to the precisely right degree. If it is too soft, the facets will become hollow when it cools. If it is not liquid enough, it cannot be sufficiently compressed and the edges of the stones will be unduly thick. Certain colored glasses, if heated too rapidly or too much, will change color.

The temperature of the die is also crucial. If the die is too cold, the surface of the glass will be shocked and develop minute surface cracks. If the die is too hot, the glass will fuse to the metal and it will be impossible to get the stones out when they are pressed.

Some sinking of the facets is inevitable, so the workman must consider which side of the stone requires the straightest facets. Then he turns that side of the die to the bottom, so that as the glass contracts upwards to the center, it will also yield downward to gravity somewhat. These two opposite tendencies cancel one another out to keep one side of the die more perfectly filled, ensuring that the stone wil be most sharply faceted on the side chosen by the craftsman—the side he was careful to place on the bottom of the mold.

When this is finished, the glass-maker still has only a rough stone. It remains to be sheared, beveled, firepolished, tablepolished and possibly foiled; each of these processes requires similarly subtle artistry. Only when all this is done will a craftsman have a perfect imitation gem.

(Otto Hoffer, *Imitation Gemstones*, East Providence, 1980)

Pressmolding in Neugablonz in 1989, done in the same traditional methods as the Gablonzers had used since the 18th century. In the background hang dozens of molding tongs, each one used to produce a differently-shaped item.

Pressmolding

In the heyday of the old glass-makers like the Schürer, the Wander and the Preussler, there was very little difference between glass-making in the Gablonz area and in neighboring Saxonia or Silesia. But the demand for small glass objects, which had grown steadily since the early 18th century, induced the makers of the Gablonz area to focus on this type of production. They began to develop new procedures for producing these small pieces in larger quantities and at lower costs, thereby finding a unique way of handling the glass and a unique niche in the market.

Above all, it was the craze for brilliant chandeliers hung with innumerable pendants which encouraged this development. Until this time, the making of chandelier pendants had been a quasi-monopoly of the French makers. To break into the market, the Bohemians needed new and more efficient procedures. The French traditionally cast their elements, while the Bohemians developed tools for *pressmolding* — squeezing the elements from a reheated glass cane. Those tools basically resemble tongs, the ends of which could be fitted with variably-shaped molds. Tools like these were used since the 18th century not only for the chandelier pendants but also for making many other small items, which soon were produced nowhere else in Europe in such diversity and such quantity.

The early tools were rather crude, leaving the glass in need of substantial additional cutting and polishing. By the mid-19th century, however, the molds ("Kappel," as they were called in Gablonz) were perfected. Since the second half of the 19th century, pressmolders were able to imprint small items — primarily buttons — with incredibly detailed patterns. With no further treatment, these pieces looked as if they were cut or engraved.

Pressmolding like this is presumed to have started around the mid-18th century. By the second half of the 18th century, indisputable documentation had been found:

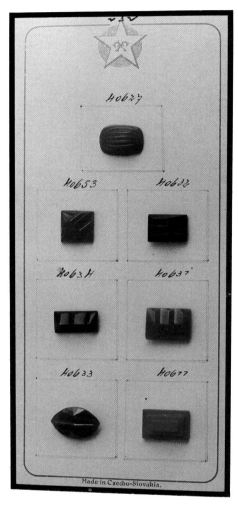

Sample card including pressmolded stones, from Fried Fréres, Gablonz, late 1920s. The stones are made from composition in classical gemstone colors: coral, onyx, carnelian and chrysoprase. The stones are molded with patterns which seem to be cut, even upon close inspection.

Button made of opalescent glass, Gablonz, early 20th century. Similar Art Nouveau patterns can be found on Gablonz buttons as early as the 1880s. In the background are covered boxes produced by the Lalique factory in the 1930s.

J1098

J1099

J1100

Close-up of a sample card, Gablonz, 1889. Three buttons in a well-balanced pattern, enhanced with hand-painted silvering. *(Courtesy of the Museum Neugablonz)*

— A treaty concluded in 1764 between the stonecutter's guild and the glass-cutter's guild, indicating that pressmolding was already a common procedure.
— Records from between 1766 and 1780 noting Hans-Georg Pfeiffer (1711-1778) and Gottfried Pfeifer in Labau as *Drücker,* i.e. "pressmolders."
— A report from Count Zinsendorf in Turnov in 1774, stating that "Some years ago, a certain Fischer has developed a tool which allows to produce the artificial jewelry much more easily and at much lower costs. The glass is drawn and squeezed into the desired shape with the help of a tong including a mold.[1]
— The records of the glass merchant Schwan, which indicate that he was selling molding tongs in 1786.

The records of the Christiansthal glassworks indicate that since 1803 they sold glass to the "glass-squeezers" ("*Glas-quetscher,*" a term to be replaced later with "*Glas-drücker*").[2] Since at least this period, pressmolding was done predominantly as it was described later, in 1877:

> In the pressmolding works [more or less standard glassworks] the glass is pressed into pendants, paperweights, inkwells, [scent] bottles and similar items...The pressmolding workshops are much smaller...they are in most cases equipped with no more but a single furnace — which is often just an open fireplace — where the canes which had been drawn from composition or glass are reheated until they are red hot to be squeezed subsequently with the help of molding tongs into buttons, beads, artificial gemstones and similar small items."[3]

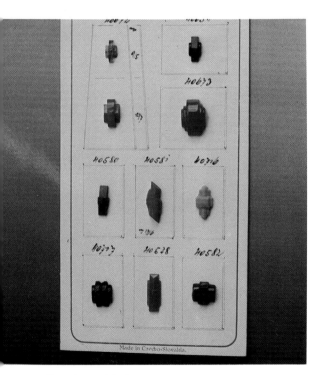

Sample card including pressmolded stones, from Fried Fréres, Gablonz, late 1920s. The stones appear to have been cut with fanciful patterns; only an expert would recognize that they were actually molded.

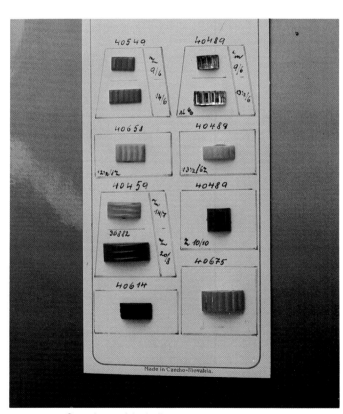

Sample card including pressmolded stones, from Fried Fréres, Gablonz, late 1920s. A collection of molded stones in classic colors, including a very fine coral variety.

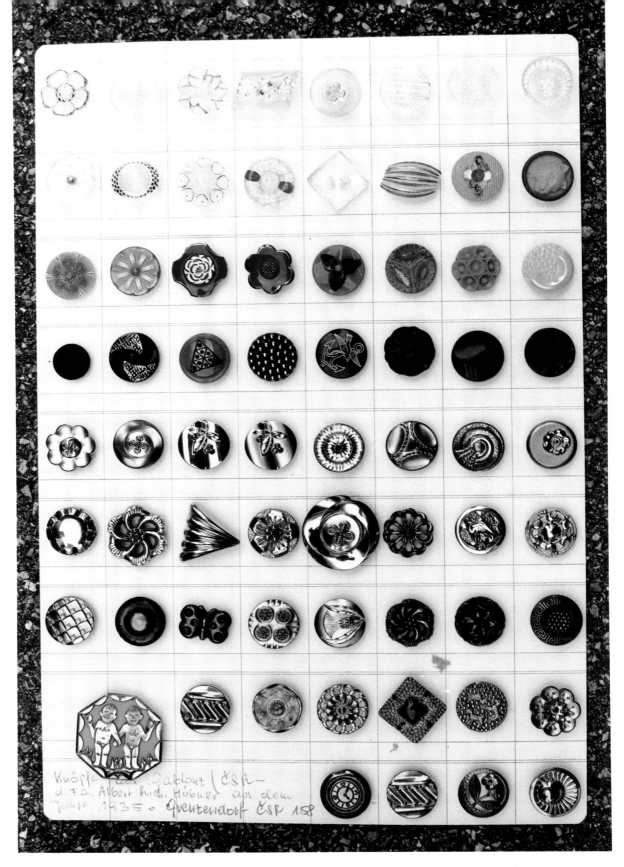

Sample card with buttons, Albert Richard Hübner, Grenzendorf, 1935. Each season required new buttons, the most prominent fashion adornment in the second half of the 19th century. The design of button molds was among the greatest challenges to the makers and engravers in Gablonz. Every button on this sample card is remarkable, but especially notable are the wildcat's head button, the butterfly button and the large "Gemini" from a series of zodiac buttons.

Brooch set with a large molded cabochon, Gablonz, 1930s. Pressmolded stones are not necessarily molded with intricate patterns. Frequently the imagination and creativity lie as much in the glass composition of the item as in the molding. In this case, a carefully marbled glass is decorated with mica. Many pressmolding craftsmen invested much time and effort in combining fanciful glasses in pleasing ways.

The humble pressmolding workshops, where several workers cooperated around a single furnace, were of central importance to the Gablonz industry. In 1856, the official statistics counted 43 pressmolding workshops in the area. Twenty years later, their number had grown to 174,[4] and in another twenty years later it had reached 225.[5] Moreover, these numbers counted only the registered and tax-paying workshops, not the hundreds of dependent workers. In 1938, in just the small village of Neudorf, there were 264 of these dependent craftsmen;[6] this figure may give a rough idea how high the total number of craftsmen, both in and out of workshops, were practicing the pressmolding profession in the Gablonz region.

Pressed or molded glass is frequently considered to be a cheap substitute for cut glass, and without doubt the impressed patterns frequently do try to approximate the patterns of cut glass. Such imitations make it easy to forget that pressmolding opened entirely new horizons of method and style for glass decoration. Capable glass-artists adapted glass to new types of handling, and joined forces with competent metal engravers who created sophisticated molds according to the patterns of inventive glass-artists. Together they developed an entirely new mode of glass design.

While the most renowned crafter of molded glass art is René Lalique, this artist had innumerable predecessors in the Gablonz industry. The inspiration for this new field of imaginative design certainly came from the button-makers. In 1835 they had already made pattered buttons from black and colored glass by using molding tongs.[7] Around the mid-19th century, jet buttons molded from black glass were one of the most important articles of the Gablonz industry. As fashion required them to become larger and larger (finally with a standard diameter up to 4 cm), it became ever more important to design their surfaces. Anyone who looks at those black Victorian buttons will soon be astonished by the glass art hidden in plain sight on the tops of those buttons. They were imprinted with tremendously fanciful and complicated patterns. In 1900, one chronicler wrote in an admiring reverie about "the sophisticated patterns on the buttons...especially those molded with cameos..."[8]

Two molded elements to be fitted into a clasp, Gablonz, before World War I.

Brooch set with a molded cabochon composed like peacock feathers. The stone is from Gablonz, while the mount is most likely from Germany, late 19th/early 20th century.

A muffchain with similarly lampworked beads, Gablonz, turn-of-the-century. To mold or lampwork such stones required labor-intensive preparation. The stones and beads include foil, and are composed of differently colored glasses. In the background is a sketch by Koloman Moser, 1898.

Glass Cameos

Long before they were created by the makers in Gablonz, glass cameos had a far-reaching history of prestige and glamour. Even in antiquity it had been a tradition to make them, either out of overlaid glass, or out of cast or molded glass. The 18th century European enthusiasm for antiquity made the popular revival of cameos a smash success.

In almost every important glass manual of the 19th century, instructions for making glass cameos can be found. Even in those manuals which say "artificial cameos are easily made,"[9] however, the instructions given reveal that the technique in general use in the 1860s was a technically complex and painstaking process. It required a plaster cast, repeated reheating in a muffle-kiln, and repeated cutting. Special attention had to be paid to the mixing of the molding clay, and molds were destroyed by the first molding process, or by one soon after. They could rarely be used for more than a few cameos. The process as described in the texts of the mid-19th century had gone virtually unchanged for three hundred years.

It took an industrial revolution in making cameos before "every maidservant could have the pleasure to wear cameo buttons."[10] Around 1870, the Gablonz makers started to produce cameos using their molding tongs. Many real artists with years of engraving experience worked so that pressmolded cameos would have the same delicacy found in high-quality genuine cameos. The best cameo engravers, including the early 20th century's Rudolf Adolf Weiss of No. 274, Kukan[11] will be remembered forever. To this very day, he is considered to have been one of the best engravers that ever lived. His cameos were sold directly to Paris to be mounted there.

In 1922 the renowned glass-technologist Wilhelm Hannich, originally from the Gablonz area, described the making of cameos:

> Cameos are again extremely fashionable. They are predominantly made in the pressmolding workshops. Only the very small cameos — those up to a diameter of 30mm — are pressmolded in one single piece. Larger cameos — up to the size of 50mm — get easily distorted or the glass does not fill up every detail of the mold. Imperfect cameos are the result. Only the very skilled workers are able to press fine cameos....The basis is often made from glass in a different color. The cameos are frequently further decorated by painting, silvering, gilding, etc. We can find white cameos on a blue or rose basis, or the heads are partly shaded in rose, blue or violet and set upon a black basis. We can find entirely black cameos as well as yellow heads upon a green polished base. Others are further decorated with stones. The basises are generally circular or rectangular and the border is polished round or cut with facets (three rows of facets). Most cameos are mounted into brooches.[12]

This description gives us a very detailed first-hand insight into the choice of cameos offered by Gablonz in the early 1920s.

Brooch including a cameo molded from black glass, further decorated with hand-painted silvering and gilding. The mount and the cameo are from Gablonz, circa 1880. Identical cameo brooches can be found in the Bijouteriemuseum in Jablonec (Gablonz) and in the Museum Neugablonz. The carefully molded head is glued upon a cut and polished base.

Two brooches with cameos in high relief. On the left, a black glass cameo molded from a lost mold; the head is glued upon the base. From Gablonz, mid 19th century; height 4.7 cm, not including the mount. On the right, a cameo of agate-colored glass, pressmolded in one piece in Neugablonz, 1950s. Large black cameos like the one on the left were originially made to compete with similar Gagat- or Lava-cameos, but since they were no easier to produce and, moreover, were heavier to wear, they were made only in limited quantities. Still, the cameo from Neugablonz proves that the making of such pieces in high relief was never completely abandoned. The Gablonz makers eventually managed to simplify the molding techniques even for this most complicated type of production.

1885.

1875.

1902.

1919.

1914.

Two brooches including cameos molded from white glass. On the left,, a cameo set on an amethyst-colored faceted stone. The cameo is from Gablonz, late 19th./early 20th century; the gold mount is probabl;y from England. On the right, a cameo set on black glass. The cameo is probably from Enns/Austria, and the mount is by Karl Stumpe, Linz/Austria, 1960s.

Brooch including a cameo molded from amethyst-colored glass, Gablonz, late 19th/early 20th centruy. The mount is possibly English. This cameo was very carefully molded, and was decorated further with metallic applications. The head is glued upon a cut and polished base which is also made from amethyst-colored glass.

Brooch including a black glass cameo assembled from two parts, Gablonz, early 20th century. The cameo was originally the central element of a bracelet, and was only later transformed into a brooch.

Two cameos from Gablonz, turn of the century. On the left, the head and the base are molded from one piece of ivory-colored glass. On the right, the cameo is composed of three elements: the head is from ivory colored glass, slightly shaded with paint; the base is made of two separate black glass pieces, which are faceted around the border.

Two brooches with cameos of identical design, Gablonz, 1920s/1930s. On the right, a head in black glass, glued upon a carnelian-colored base. The mount is secondary, assembled from assorted elements from different periods. On the left, a Bakelite cameo molded in one piece. The mount is also secondary. This cameo design appears quite frequently on the market, also in button form, and generally in plastic.

Two cameos, each molded in one piece, Gablonz, 1910/1920. On the left, opaque white glass accentuated with paint. On the right, Bakelite.

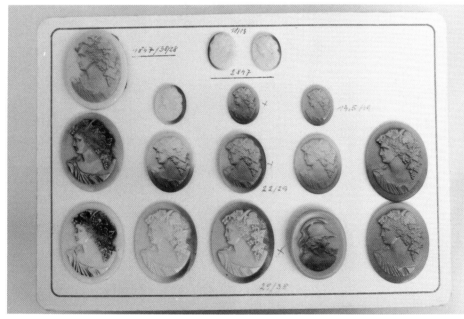

Sample card with cameos, from Neugablonz, 1971, by Wilhelm G. Wildner. The tradition of making fine pressmolded cameos continued after World War II primarily in Neugablonz. *(Courtesy of Museum Neugablonz)*

Selection of pins set with "hematite" stones, Gablonz, early 20th century. Most of the molded stones were made to resemble intaglio-cut stones.

Lampworking

Lampworking, a crucial glassmaking technique, consists of reheating glass tubes or canes with the aid of a special lamp in order to rework them into new designs. These lamps burn gas to heat the glass until it becomes malleable. The softened glass can be twisted or pressed into a wide range of forms.

Blown beads

Among the cottage workers excel the bead-blowers. Their skillfully blown beads are completed by the bead-liners...easily recognizable by their darkened skin which is caused by the silver solution which they suck into the beads. The finishing and the stringing of the beads is done by the women and children of the family." (Gustav Leutelt, 1932)

Gablonz lampwork artisans took up bead-blowing at the end of the 18th century, when such beads were in strong demand. One early bead-blower of the region was a certain Endler (1760 - ?), also a pressmolder. Other bead-blowers in the early 19th century included Johann Hemrich, Josef Scheibler, Anton and Anastas Seidel and Anton Appelt. During this period, blown beads were made either from colored composition or

A costume including such a crown, Northern Germany, 19th century.

Bridal crown from Germany composed of blown beads, late 18th/early 19th century. In this era, blown beads were made primarily in Thuringia or Gablonz. *(Courtesy of Germanisches Nationalmuseum, Nürnberg)*

Black blown beads molded with facets, from Gablonz, late 19th/early 20th century. Beads blown with facets are documented since the 1820s.

from crystal. Their color was frequently intensified by lining, and even at this early stage they were made in many fancy shapes.[1] During the first third of the 19th century, blown beads reckoned among the most profitable export items for Gablonz. Their great importance can also be deduced from the fact that in 1830 the prominent glass merchant Heinrich Göble sent samples of such beads to the *Nationalproduktenkabinett* in Vienna, in a collection which comprised only the finest products of the Austrian monarchy.

Due to the quickly growing economic importance of these beads, makers developed many different methods for producing an endless variety of them during the first half of the 19th century. In addition to the luxury beads blown individually from colored composition and decorated with paint, the makers blew standard beads from crystal which were made attractive by a simple lining process. The metallic lining which produced "mirror beads" (*Spiegelperlen*) was known in Gablonz since the late 18th century.[2]

Around the mid-19th century, the choice of blown beads expanded to include a great variety of mold-blown beads (blown into wooden molds) shaped like organic objects, including pears, acorns, olives and melons. Around 1874, beadblowing was considerably simplified when the Josefsthal metalworker Pitzek constructed a metal mold which allowed craftsmen to blow up to eight beads simultaneously. Nonetheless, beadblowing remained a labour-intensive job, requiring much skill. The work was usually undertaken by women cottage workers.

Each season, a different type of blown bead came into fashion. Around 1850, no bead sold better than the large black faceted bead, but by 1870 everybody wanted melon-ribbed and silver-lined beads, and not a single black bead. Notwithstanding changing fashions, two types became standard after the late 18th century: mirror beads lined with metallic solutions, and artificial pearls lined (and later coated) with a solution made of fish scales.

Between 1880 and 1895 the demand for metal-lined beads grew so high that the Gablonz area supported approximately 2000 bead-blowers. In addition to the standard silver-lined beads, Gablonz provided "gold"-lined beads made with solutions containing copper. Then, in 1898, Iwan Weiskopf introduced a process for lining the beads with real gold, another advantage for the Gablonz industry.

Gold-lined blown beads, and a hat pin including two blown beads, from Gablonz, late 19/early 20th century.

Lady wearing a necklace of blown "pearls," Germany, 1913.

Watch-chain with one blown "pearl" and several gold-lined blown beads, from Gablonz, late 19th/early 20th century.

Lady wearing a similar watch-chain, Germany, early 20th century.

In 1906, however, Gablonz began to gradually lose the market for silver-lined beads—which had been such a tremendous economic success—to Japanese competitors. The number of beadblowers working in Gablonz dropped sharply. After World War One the competition from the Far East lessened, and since the Gablonzers had maintained their virtual monopoly on gold-lined beads through silver's slow period they were able to recover. The number of bead-blowers quickly increased to about a thousand, at which point the industry stabilized.

Ear pendants composed of blown beads, from Gablonz in the first third of the 20th century.

Necklace and brooch including coral-colored "spun" beads and a large stone. From Gablonz, of uncertain date.

A bouquet brooch composed of lampworked flowers, from Gablonz, 1920s/1930s.

Glass-spinning

Strictly speaking, spun glass is glass reduced to thin threads and then worked into fabrics. Such glass threads were already being made in the Gablonz area, in Thuringia and in Murano/Venice around the 1820s,[3] but articles manufactured from spun glass became a real craze only after 1873, when Jules de Brunfaut (1819 - ?) launched a collection of spun glass products at the Vienna World Fair. For about twenty years it remained extremely fashionable to have accessories like hats and cushions made from spun glass.

In Bohemia, the designation "glass-spinning" (*Glasspinnerei*) was also applied to a craft which is better referred to as "freehand lampworking," which was practiced primarily in Murano/Venice. There are no reliable and detailed records to be found about this craft in the area of Gablonz. There are, however, brief references to "flowers and figurines" which were made in the early 19th century in the Gablonz area,[4] and to the "flower bouquets" shown by the Gablonz industry at the World Fair in Vienna in 1873. These references indicate that lampworking "in the Venetian style," as it was called, was practised in the area at least since the early 19th century.

Another bouquet brooch of similar origin.

Necklace including fragile spun beads, Gablonz, late 1920s.

Most helpful in this context are the records of families which had a lampworking tradition, such as the Blaschkas from Liebenau. One member of this family worked between 1840 and 1870 with the famous Baccarat glassworks in France, where he most likely created lampwork paperweights. Two other Blaschkas created stunning lampworked flowers and animals, for which they became known in the United States.

Sample card with molded stones including lampworked flowers; by Schuhmeier of Neugablonz, 1960s. The craftsman continues the lampworking tradition of his father Franz Schuhmeier (1907-1968).

Florian Pattermann

Another family with a strong reputation for lampworking was the Pattermann family. The first recorded glass-spinner in this family was Karl Pattermann (1754 - ?), a glass-maker at the Zenkerglassworks in Antoniwald. Later, he ran his own composition workshop in Polaun. Of his five children, two — Carl (1797- 1877) and Florian (1808 - 1899) — became renowned lampworkers. During the1830s and 1840s, Carl excelled primarily as a successful businessman. He showed various lampworked products ranging from beads to toys in important exhibitions, such as the one in Prague in 1836 or the one in Vienna in 1845, and he was awarded many prizes. Remarkably, he is said to have sold "annually circa 28,000 glass boxes and 40,000 glass toys — above all to the Netherlands."[5] To judge by the products lampworked by this family that have survived through the years, Bohemian lampworking closely resembled Thuringian lampworking; makers in both areas liked to use twisted filigree canes. Florian Pattermann also used twisted filigree canes predominantly, especially for decorating glass boxes and other items.

Few fragile items have survived through the centuries, so it is difficult to catalogue thoroughly the varieties of freehand lampworking as it was practiced in Gablonz. The only documentation left for modern historians and collectors are the many "spun" buttons and beads, which were generally finished with some molding.

A bowl with lampworked decoration by Florian Pattermann of Gablonz, 1868.

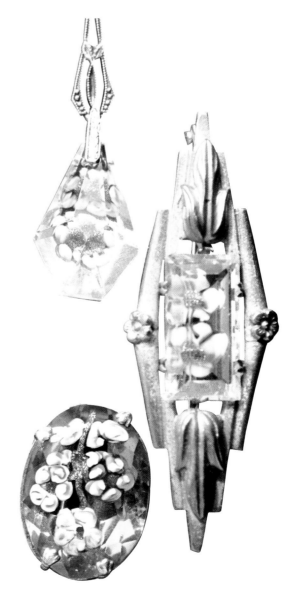

Two brooches and a pendant with faceted stones decorated with floral lampwork patterns. From Gablonz, 1920/1930s.

including a molded stone with
railings. From Gablonz, late 19th/
century.

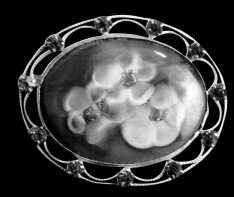

Brooch including a molded st
lampworked floral decoration. From
late 19th/early 20th century.

Necklace and brooch including stones with
lampworked floral decorations. Necklace:
Gablonz, 1930s or later. Brooch: Jablonec,
modern.

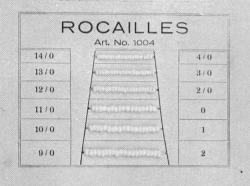

ROCAILLES
Art. No. 1004

14 / 0		4 / 0
13 / 0		3 / 0
12 / 0		2 / 0
11 / 0		0
10 / 0		1
9 / 0		2

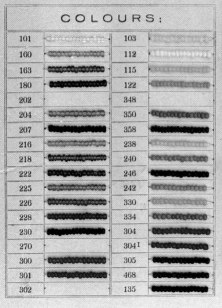

COLOURS:

101	103	
160	112	
163	115	
180	122	
202	348	
204	350	
207	358	
216	238	
218	240	
222	246	
225	242	
226	330	
228	334	
230	304	
270	304 I	
300	305	
301	468	
302	135	

A sample card of "Rocailles" from Gablonz, of uncertain period. *(Courtesy of the Museum Neugablonz*

Two samples of beadwork made from "Rocailles": (above) African beadwork from the early 20th century; (below) German beadwork from the mid-19th century. These beautiful abstract patterns are evidence of similar design sensibilities, despite the great distance separating the two craftsmen responsible for these pieces.

Beads

Called "*Sprengperlen*" (cut beads) among the Gablonz makers of the early 19th century, drawn beads were the most successful invention in the history of beads. At long last, beads did not have to be made one by one; instead, they were cut from bunches of glass tubes. This procedure was developed in Murano and Venice to almost industrial standards, allowing mass production of perfect beads to a degree never before possible.

It was not just the efficiency of high-volume production that made these beads successful, but also the new ability to produce beads in every possible size, down to miniscule dimensions. They became a standard decoration for textiles worldwide, ornamenting materials with their never-fading brilliance. Because of the tremendous economic success of these beads, many countries in Europe tried to establish their own bead-making industries, but Murano and Venice managed to maintain a virtual monopoly well into the 19th century. The term "Venetian beads" was still used to refer to small drawn beads even in the mid-19th century.

In the Gablonz area, the drawn bead industry could begin to compete with Murano only in the second half of the 19th century, even though they had long been manufacturing "Korallen" in the Isermountains. In German-speaking areas, simple beads manufactured in mass quantity were called "Korallen" to distinguish them from blown beads.

In 1740, the Grünwald glassworks produced plain black beads,[1] most likely simple wound beads made according to basic procedures developed in antiquity. Also in that century, Bohemians made composition beads — mostly colored like garnets — which were used primarily for rosaries; the French, lacking the technology to make colored glass themselves, used these beads to shade their enamels.[2] Still, these widely distributed beads were not drawn beads.

The making of drawn beads in North Bohemia is noted for the first time in the late 18th century, in Morchenstern and Neudorf.[3] It is likewise noted that the Riedel glassworks in Neuwiese and Christiansthal and the Unger glassworks in Tiefenbach sold tubes in 1790 and in 1800. Whether those tubes were meant for beadblowers or beadcutters is not recorded. In the early years of this production line, the beads were cut within the glassworks, but soon the glassworks began to sell their tubes to independent cutters. At first the cutters lived close to the glassworks, in the Kamnitzvalley or in Johannesberg. By and by, however, the tedious work — done mostly by farmers to suplement their incomes — moved south. It went through Morchenstern and Labau, and by 1870 finally settled in the Czech villages south of the Schwartzbrunnkamm (the mountain ridge separating German-speaking regions from those that spoke Czech).

The earliest drawn beads were cut from round tubes, but in the 19th century the tubes began to be molded with six to eight sides, thus giving the beads a basic set of facets. The Gablonz bead industry enjoyed its first boom season in the 1820s. The Riedel factory in Klein-Iser was founded solely to satisfy the growing need for tubes and canes.

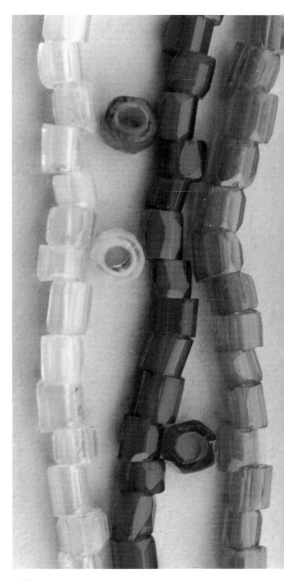

Three strands of drawn beads from Gablonz, 19th century. Beads of this sort are known among trade bead collectors as "Russian beads," though makers called them *Sprengperlen*.

At the 1829 exhibition of Bohemian products in Prague, a chronicler admired the beauty of the faceted beads made from tubes, as well he might. While the lampworked beads were mostly made from composition, these drawn beads were made from glass. The faceting of these early beads was completed, one bead at a time, with hand-driven devices operated by cottage workers. The chronicler ought to have admired the Bohemians' industriousness, too; these beads were exported from Gablonz at the rate of no less than 2.4 billion a year.[4]

Despite having such an active bead industry in the first half of the 19th century, it seems as if Gablonz had not yet started to compete directly with Murano in the production of "Rocailles," small beads cut from round tubes and then finished by reheating. Instead, they continued to cut their beads from relatively large tubes until the 1840s, finishing them and smoothing the ends by cutting them, or by tumbling them with an abrasive. Manufacturer Josef Pfeiffer made the first try to enter the promising Rocailles business in 1847, and in 1856 such beads were offered at the New York World Fair by renowned exporters Josef Keil of Gablonz and Blaschka & Söhn of Liebenau.[5]

This bead business began a period of great success beginning in the 1870s. Several new glassworks were founded in those years solely to supply tubes and canes, and the area counted between two and three thousand beadcutters. The demand for glass tubes was so overwhelming that glass had to be brought in from other areas as well, including the glassworks near Teplitz (Teplice), from Moravia, and even from Murano.

In those years, Ludwig Breit founded a family business which was to become one of the most important ones of its field in Gablonz. In 1868, Ludwig and Hartwig Breit had first opened a glassworks in Wiesenthal, limiting its production exclusively to buttons. A little while later they founded another Ludwig Breit factory in Wiesenthal, where they produced Rocailles from tubes they drew themselves.

Until the 1880s, the beads were cut solely by human cutters, but the heavy competition of foreign bead industries made it necessary to introduce cutting machines. As one commentator noted, progress in Gablonz could no longer be limited to innovative patterns of design, but must grow to include advanced methods of production as well. "The future of our industry," he wrote, "depends on this."[6] The sudden success of French and German "Oriental" beads (see Porcelain Beads section) had a heavily adverse effect on the Gablonz trade for seven years before the Redlhammers could respond properly to their challenge; this had taught the bead manufacturers from Gablonz how easily one could lose important shares of the market.

Thousands of beadcutters were made "redundant" by this mechanization; these workers became part of a number of bloody uprises. Despite this upset, though, it cannot be denied that industrialization had become necessary. Bohemian production costs had become twice as

The Ludwig Breit bead factory in Wiesenthal, 1913.

expensive as those in Murano, where bead makers had been introduced to the first simple cutting machines in the 1820s. The Gablonzers were able to overcome Murano's head start, and to overcome further difficulties of progress in future years. Perhaps their resilience was rooted in their willingness to surpass the selection offered by their competitors; Gablonz bead collections did not merely imitate the Muranese offerings, but also provided new and complementary pieces.

The Breit company had to extend its premises continually, and in 1912 they inaugurated a new bead factory. After World War I they produced not only tubes for their own beadmaking use, but also canes for other area makers and "ballottini" for industrial use. Ballottini, glass globes of microscopic dimensions, were mainly used for reflecting surfaces.

After the expulsion, Ludwig Breit, Jr. cooperated with other glassmakers from Gablonz to build up a glass industry, beginning in 1947. They located their new center in Schwäbisch-Gmünd. Breit renewed his family traditions within the Ludwig Breit Wiesenthalhütte glassworks in this town.

Porcelain Beads

Towards the end of the 1870s, the European market was flooded with what were known as "agate" buttons and beads, which would eventually be called "Oriental beads," "Bapterosse beads" or "Porcelain beads"; among English-speaking trade bead collectors, they are called "tile beads." They were extremely cheap, an important factor in this zipperless period. Fashion frequently required buttons in great quantity, but not necessarily with great ornamentation, as on shirts and underwear.

New products like these were a serious threat to various traditional types of beads and buttons. They were made not from glass but from a porcelain-likle substance, and were molded and fired in a process similar to that used for porcelain. These buttons came ready-made out of the kiln, requiring no further treatment. Customers appreciated the large hole, but most of all they were pleased that neither buttons nor beads of this porcelain material had the sharp edges glass items did; buttons of glass had an annoying tendency to cut the threads with which they had been sewn to a garment.

The main suppliers of these beads and buttons, covering the entire European market, were Rister & Co. in Freiburg, Germany, and F. Bapterosse in Paris, France.[7]

The manufacturers in Gablonz had nothing to offer that was similar to these porcelain-like beads and buttons. But after the initial shock, the Redlhammer brothers — Albert (1858-1937) and Eduard (1857-1948) — filled the gap, offering their own variety of porcelain-like beads by 1885. They developed by themselves the mixture from which the beads were made, as well as the necessary machinery. The Redlhammers were

Letterhead of the Redlhammer bead factory.

Porzellanperlen- und Knopffabrik

Gebrüder Redlhammer

R. G.

Gablonz (Neiße)

awarded many prizes at various exhibitions, including a gold medal at the 1900 Paris World Fair. Around the turn of the century, the company employed about 350 workers and about 1000 cottage workers.

In 1911 the Redlhammers expanded their production with a large, modern premises in the Hüttenstrasse. This was an important investment, made possible by an agreement Eduard Ludwig Redlhammer had initiated between the important European manufacturers of this particular type of goods. The agreement lasted from 1909 to 1945, regulating the conditions of sale and payment, prices, and the quantities to be produced by each manufacturer.

Eduard Ludwig had founded an additional company, Eduard Ludwig Redlhammer & Söhne, in 1920. They supplied the bijouterie industry with high-quality canes in such major colors as coral and amber. They also held a patent for a special variety of satin glass.

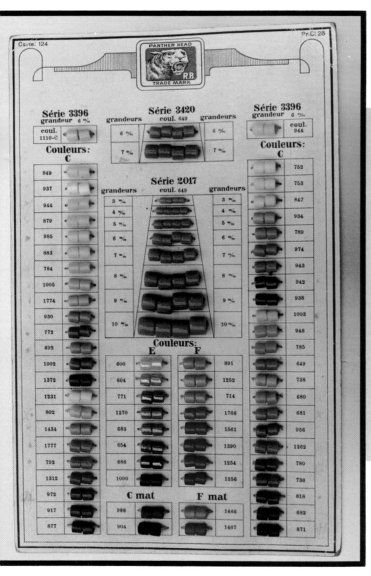

A sample card of porcelain beads, from the pre-war period. *(Courtesy of the Museum Neugablonz)*

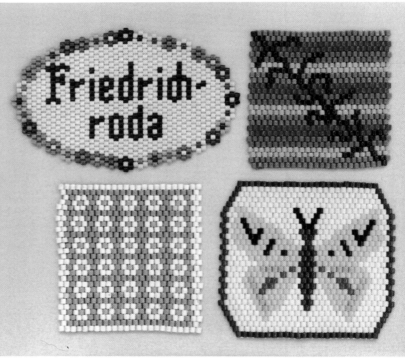

Four table-mats made of porcelain beads, from Germany, 1930s.

Buttons

Glass buttons mounted on metal bases were made in the Iser mountains since the 18th century, and lampworked buttons began to be made in the first third of the 19th century, if not earlier. But since Bohemian exporters showed a large selection of beads and stones but no buttons at their exhibition in Prague in 1829, it is obvious that button-making had not yet become financially important to the area. It would appear that Gablonz button production was unable to grow to significant proportions until the late 1820s, when craftsmen mastered the incorporation of metal shanks into glass. The composition-maker Josef Scheibler is said to have developed compatible composition in the 1820s, allowing workers to combine metal and glass without fear that the glass would crack as it cooled.[1]

Buttons — the costume jewels of the 19th century

Metal buttons incorporating colored glass elements, from Gablonz, 19th century. Buttons of this type were made beginning in the later 18th century. In the early 19th century, the Jäckel company provided the button industry with glass elements like these.

The Jäckel company is said to have been the first Gablonz manufacturer to market buttons with incorporated metal shanks on a large scale, beginning in 1825.[2] They had most likely initiated the necessary experimental work, since for many years they had been the main supplier of ornamental glass elements to the German button industry. Buttons with metal shanks — either wound or pressmolded — could thus be made in greater quantities starting in the 1830s. Still, the button industry began its drastic expansion only around 1860, when fashions began to demand their products in great supply. Button-making soon became a dominant branch of the Gablonz industry, with manufacturers concentrated in Morchenstern, Wiesenthal and Gablonz.

The growing demand was responsible for major technical changes in the 1870s. Buttons were given loop shanks with metal backplates, which allowed the shanks to be more securely embedded in the glass. Since 1875 the standard pressmolded buttons could be made without additional cutting and polishing because sharper and more precise molds were available. These pressmolded buttons could be finished with firepolishing alone. Until the 1870s most buttons had been made from black glass, but as the demand for fashionable buttons grew the craftsmen learned to press them from all types of colored glass.

1868

1875

1871

1882. Coatbuttons: the larger, the better.

1889. "Austrian Tinies."

Buttons sliced from a patterned glass cane.
From Gablonz, mid-19th century

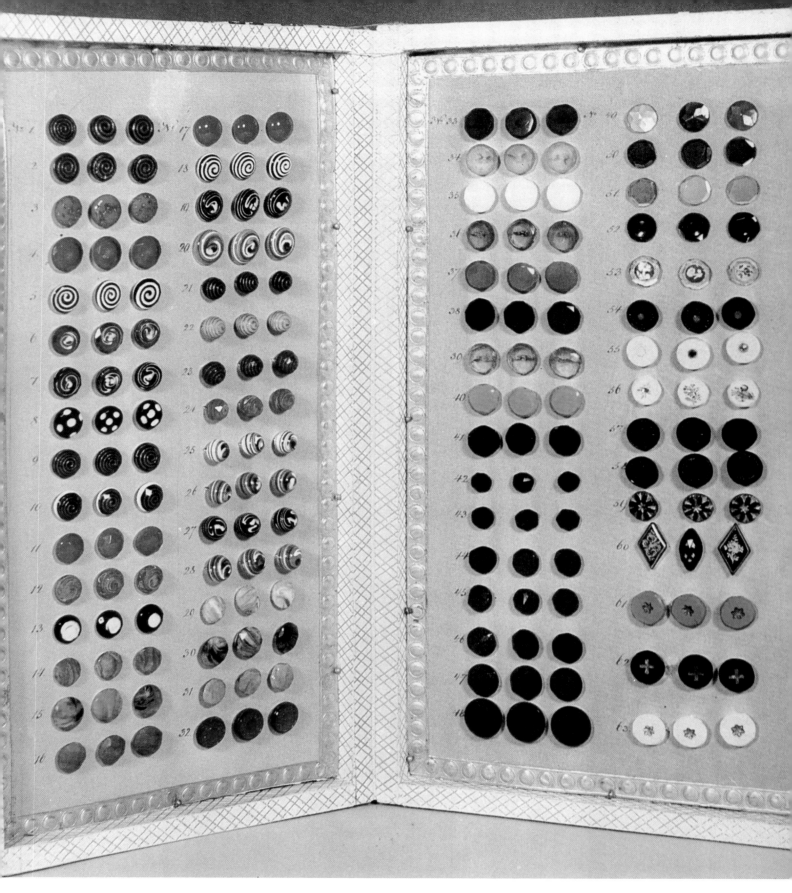

Sample card with buttons from Gablonz, 19th
century. The sample card was put together by
the Unger export company. *(Courtesy of the
Technical Museum, Vienna)*

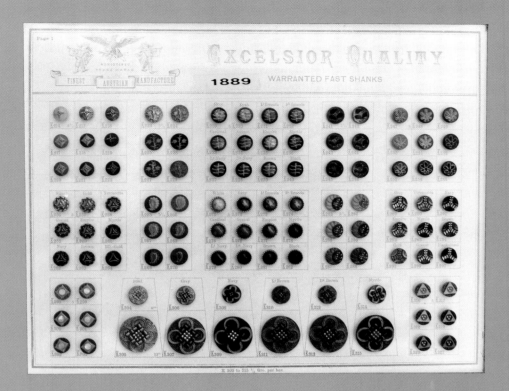

Sample card with pressmolded dress and mantle buttons, from Gablonz, 1889. *(Courtesy of the Museum Neugablonz)*

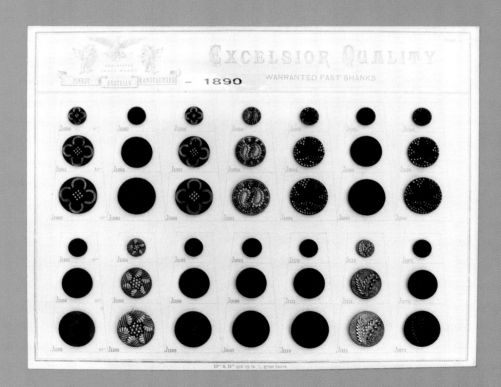

Sample card with pressmolded dress and mantle buttons, from Gablonz, 1890. *(Courtesy of the Museum Neugablonz)*

The demand for buttons was not constant, however; it depended largely on the vagaries of fashion. Since the 1860s, each decade had seasons of high demand for buttons but also seasons in which it was extremely low. The periods which strongly favored the button industry in the 19th century were 1865-67, 1870-74, 1878-86 and 1894-95.[3] By and large the buttons were made by inidividual cottage workers, but because of these periods of high demand four button factories were founded in the 1880s.

In the 20th century, buttons remained an important article for the Gablonz industry. In the 1920s, button-makers worked in almost every village around Gablonz, though production was more concentrated in Morchenstern, Wiesenthal and Gablonz itself. Each of these centers had about twenty makers. Places like Grenzendorf and Johannesberg followed closely, each with more than a dozen button-makers.

Three lampworked buttons covered with green trailings, from Gablonz, early 20th century. The making of these buttons was very time-consuming. The have a globular crystal core, which is closely entwined with a green twisted cane.

6006   6170

A close-up of some Gablonz lampworked buttons similar to the fancy vest buttons on page 74, from the early 20th century. Fancy trailings like these were among the most popular button decorations applied by the Gablonz lampworkers since the late 19th century.

Black pressmolded buttons, Gablonz, late 19th century. Such small black buttons are frequently called "Austrian Tinies." They are decorated with patterns just as elaborate and fanciful as the larger buttons are.

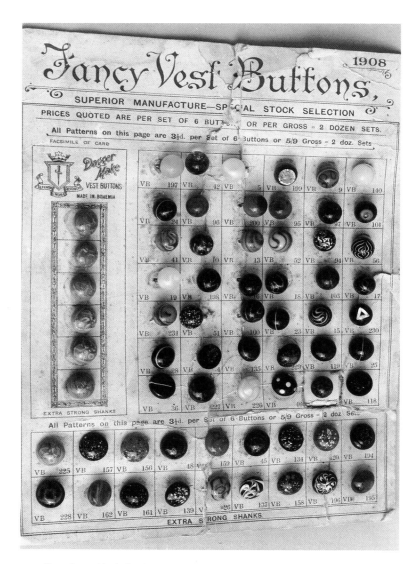

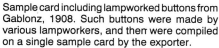

Sample card including lampworked buttons from Gablonz, 1908. Such buttons were made by various lampworkers, and then were compiled on a single sample card by the exporter.

A metal button with a plastic pressmolded element, made in Gablonz in the early 20th century. The button is impressed with an intricate pattern: an apple on a branch, with a knife cutting into the apple.

"Mother-of-pearl" buttons by Hübner in Grenzendorf, 1930-1935. These buttons were made from molded crystal, coated with the same method that artificial pearls were. They were manufactured successfully in Gablonz beginning in the 1870s.

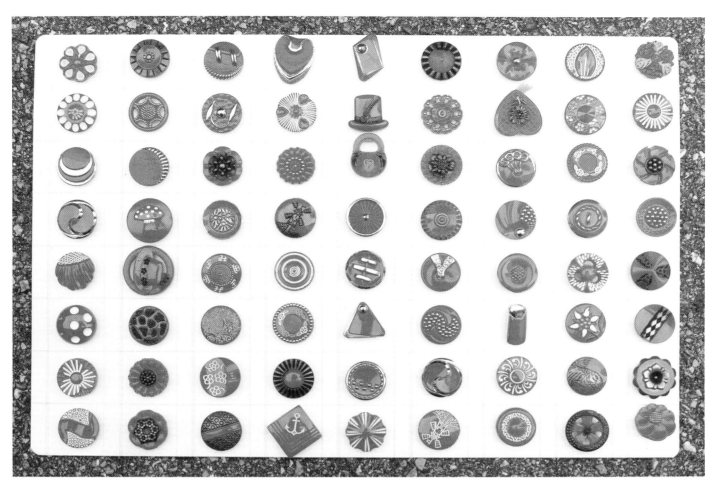

A sample card with red pressmolded buttons by Hübner in Grenzendorf, 1930-1935. *(Courtesy of the Museum Neugablonz)*

Fancy buttons pressmolded from ivory-colored glass; they are further decorated with paint. By Hübner in Grenzendorf, 1930-1935. *(Courtesy of the Museum Neugablonz)*

Metal buttons with glass stones, from Gablonz,
late 19th and early 20th centuries.

Metal buttons decorated with strass, Gablonz,
first third of the 20th century.

Lampworked "paperweight" buttons from Gablonz, early 20th century. The buttons have a four-way metal shank, as they were made in the late 19th and early 20th centuries. The making of these buttons was extremely labor-intensive: a layer of satin glass was decorated with carefully arranged glass bits, which were then encircled with three loops of glass filament. The entire arrangement was covered with crystal, which was finally molded with three indentations.

Metalworking

The Gürtler are craftsmen similar to goldsmiths; both assemble metal elements into jewelry which is frequently decorated with stones. In the past, the term "jewelry" included such adornments as shoe buckles, buttons and belts (*Gürtel*) — the term from which the title of those craftsmen is derived. What distinguishes the Gürtler from the goldsmiths are the types of metal which each was permitted to use: goldsmiths were restricted to precious metals, the Gürtler to nonprecious metals and silver (thought they could silver and gild all their creations). From the beginning, however, each trespassed on the other's professional territory from time to time, thus violating the rules of their governing bodies. The Gürtler sometimes worked gold and silver, the precious metals; the goldsmiths sometimes used copper and brass. In 1652, a Nuremberg goldsmith made a copper girdle, and was sued by the Gürtler! This was typical of the constant bickering between the two groups, which had reached even into the Highest Court by 1670.[1]

The fact that the Gürtler handle primarily nonprecious metals has sometimes made people look down upon them, ignoring the fact that the skills and craftsmanship demanded from a Gürtler is identical to that which a goldsmith must have. The German bourgeois of the late 19th and early 20th centuries yearned for nothing but the "real" thing — gold or silver jewelry, no matter how insignificant the design or craftsmanship of the piece. Only fashionable ladies in European capitals, and some in America, appreciated the decorative value of well-designed "fancy" jewelry at this stage.

The French philosopher Montaigne discussed the desire "to put adornment within everybodies' reach" in the 16th century, praising the accomplishments of the Gürtler of his era, who had revolutionized the wearing of jewelry. They made jewelry a privilege not only of the rich, but also of the common people. The Gürtlers from Gablonz were instrumental in this jewelry revolution.

Jewelry was first made in the Gablonz area in the mid-18th century. The earliest products were made primarily from silver, and included pieces like chains composed from coins, shoe buckles, applications for pipes and walking sticks, and ear pendants of silver filigree. In the second half of the 18th century, jewelry was made from metals like copper and tombac, created either by Gürtler or by "Compositions-Galanteriearbeiter" (as those craftsmen who were not members of the guild were called).[2] Chasing from brass and casting of tin were the two basic manufacturing techniques.

An important element of their work was the pointed setting, crafted with many prongs to hold the stones. Such settings were assembled into all sorts of decorations, mainly for hats and the hair; they were also composed into crucifix pendants. Studs and shirt buttons were also widely used, and for them the makers assembled just two such settings. This jewelry got a bright surface from acid dips, hand polishing and "cold" silverplating. Casting from tin was mainly used for buttons.

This early bijouterie from Gablonz was bought by merchants from trading capitals like Nuremberg or Augsburg. The costume jewelry trade was already of considerable economic importance for Bohemia. Thirteen percent of the glass export gains were derived from the bijouterie of Turnau, Liebenau and Gablonz.[3] The names of various Gürtler from Gablonz began to appear in the early 19th century — for example,

A stamped filigree brooch set with stones in many colors, from Gablonz, 1920s/1930s. There is a certain link between the designs of this brooch and that of the top, left, page 78; here, however, the naturalistic features have been abstracted. This brooch has characteristics which are considered to be typical of the ornate Bohemian bijouterie.

A photograph of a lady with a stamped filigree brooch. From Germany, 1885.

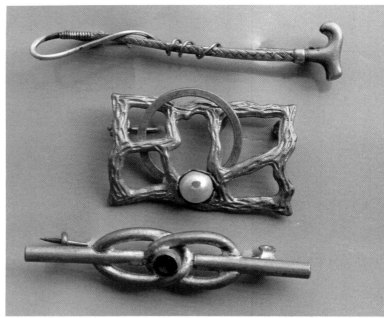

Two brooches made from tombac and brass, from Gablonz, 1870s and 1880s. The upper brooch is made of naturalistic flowers, encircled by stamped filigree. The lower brooch also incorporates natural themes, including a bird.

Three brooches made from tombac, Gablonz, late 19th century. These are very much in accordance with the general jewelry trends of the day.

Two brooches resembling bunches of grapes, from Gablonz, late 19th century. The hundreds of Gürtler in Gablonz made jewelry not only in the ornate stamped filigree considered typical of Bohemian jewelry, but also to fit every possibly trend of the international market. During the late 19th century, fruit clusters like these were in great demand. They were made by all jewelers, from renowned goldsmiths in cosmopolitan centers to unknown Gürtlers in remote Gablonz villages.

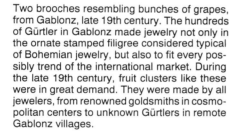

A brooch shaped like a bunch of grapes. From Gablonz, late 19th century. The overall design and the extremely naturalistic leaves are typical of 19th century jewelry. While stamped leaves and flowers like these survived in Gablonz bijouterie into the 20th century, they gradually became more abstract in design.

Hieronymous Hoffmann, a maker of brass rings, in 1800, and the brothers Vinzenz and Felix Heidrich, owners of a pipe application factory, in 1810.

In the early 19th century, it became quite customary in the Habsburg monarchy to wear artificial jewelry. These items were made from tombac, bronze or brass wires, partly set with gemstones to make them look like "real" jewelry. Popular items included rings, ear pendants, fob chains, seals, brooches, pendants, colliers, diadems and haircombs.[4]

Tombac in reddish and yellowish shades became the most succesful subtitute for gold. Eventually, a "fire-gilding" process came into use for treating tombac, brass and copper; this bonded precious metals like gold to the non-precious base metals.

In 1824 a chronicler reported that the bijouterie from Gablonz had not yet attained the quality of that manufactured in England, France or Germany.[5] This evaluation is certainly related to the fact that at this point Gablonz makers still followed their own design lines very closely. They did not imitate "real" jewelry forms in an attempt to deceive the buyer, a practice widely complained of elsewhere.

Around 1820, the manufacturer Philip Pfeiffer brought to Gablonz two Gürtler from Idar-Oberstein, a German town much renowned for its jewelry. More soon followed, including Peter Sarder and Franz Klaar. Those makers were well-acquainted with taste and fashions in Western Europe, and sparked the expansion of Gablonz's bijouterie industry. During the 1820s, the number of Gürtler in Gablonz rose from about two dozen to more than fifty, nine of whom were craftsmen originally from Idar-Oberstein "whose products compared well with the French jewelry."[6]

Inspired by attentive tradesmen who consistently brought news from the western capitals to the remote Gablonz, inventive local Gürtler began to improve their techniques. A major breakthrough in the field came in the early 1830s: the Gürtler Anton Rössler, in close cooperation with the mechanic Kajetan Schier, developed the first tools for making stamped elements . These were elaborate elements from which the final Gürtler work could be assembled. Also during the 1830s, French bijouterie-makers tried to become independent from their German suppliers in the *semilor* market—the manufacturing of jewelry from alloys that resembled gold. The French also began experimenting on their own with stamped elements for the first time.[7]

An advertisement for the Gürtler cooperative in Gablonz, from the turn of the century. In addition to the jewelry and other metal items made by the Gürtler, this picture displays technical devices of central importance to the profession, including the stamping press in the middle, and two elements for electroplating at the left.

Stamping and cutting tools necessary for achieving perfect stamped elements. The quality of the elements depends not only on the designer's creativity and the engraver's craftsmanship, but also on the skill of the metalworker who makes the cutting tool. These tools must match the filigree patterns with utmost precision.

Various elements of Gürtler-work. Some parts of the stamped elements look as if they were made of wire. Due to the skill of the metal-worker, this stamped filigree pattern has been faultlessly cut. *(Courtesy of Ernst Seidel, Warmensteinach)*

Sample card with small stamped element. The company Josef Hillebrand (b.1865-1931). The estampery was founded in 1898. These pieces made circa 1920.

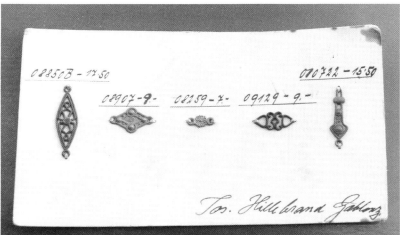

Two stamped elements from an important estampery, 1930s.

A modern stamping tool, engraved with a Gürtler-work pattern. *(Courtesy of Ernst Seidel of Warmensteinach)*

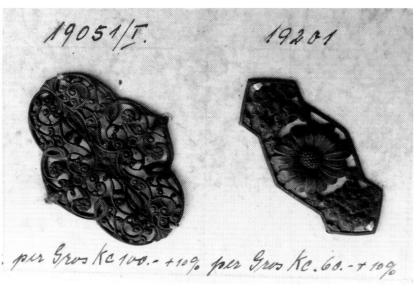

The stamping of the elements. This metal has been cut into strips as wide as the required piece; it is now stamped with the basic pattern. *(Courtesy of Ernst Seidel, Warmensteinach)*

The soldering of the elements. Depending on the design and the number of elements, it can take between ten and twelve soldering steps to assemble an entire piece. The more three-dimensional the design is, the more difficult it is to arrange the elements for soldering.

The enameling of the bijouterie. After this step comes the gilding or silvering of the piece; on high-quality work, this is done through electro-plating. Next comes the careful polishing of the piece. *(Courtesy of Ernst Seidel, Warmensteinach)*

Setting the stones. This tiresome work is traditionally the domain of women.

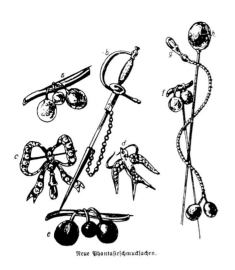

An illustration: the latest in novelty jewelry, Germany, 1890.

Though ready-made stamped pieces would later replace not only such techniques as chasing and casting but also filigree, the earliest of them were still as simple as the prefabricated elements used by the gold- and silversmiths. Only after several decades would the gradually perfected tools allow craftsmen to achieve the fragile, filigree-like elements which would become a virtual trademark of Gablonz bijouterie. In the 1830s, filigree still had to be done in the traditional, labor-intensive way, with many keen-eyed workers assembling many delicate wires. Any stamped element required the skill and the creativity of good engravers, however. These craftsmen prepared the fanciful and detailed patterned stamps, which then required the precise work of good metalworkers to make exactly matching cutting tools. Thus, the expansion and the transformation of the Gürtler industry in Gablonz began to draw from surrounding areas a new group of settlers, workmen skilled in these crafts.

While in 1829 the Gablonz bijouterie was not considered interesting enough to be shown at the Bohemian craft and manufacturing exhibition in Prague, the new process brought the Gablonzers into a leading industry position. Between the 1840s and 1870s, their share of the fashionable goods market grew rapidly, borne by an increasingly experienced and proficient export business.

The European bourgeois followed the capital cities' fashion rules strictly. French design ranked at the top of this scale, and no European manufacturer of fashionable goods would have dared to launch a fashion contradicting the Paris trends; makers closely followed the French patterns. Gablonz makers began to adapt to this restriction in the early 19th century. Their early Gürtler work had been based on traditional patterns, but as they turned toward the world market of fashionable jewelry they found that buying prefabricated elements from

An advertisement for Franz J. Jantsch's Gablonz company.

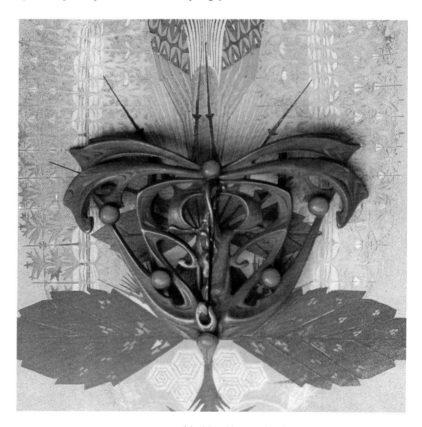

A belt buckle set with chrysoprase glass stones, from turn-of-the-century Gablonz. Art Nouveau designs were produced in abundance to satisfy a voracious market.

A photograph of a lady wearing a portrait pin, from Germany, 1910.

A portrait pin and a portrait pendant, from turn-of-the-century Gablonz. These articles were mass-produced.

Two heart-shaped brooches from Gablonz, late 19th/early 20th century. The left brooch is enameled (though the enamel has worn off of the violet), and the right brooch is set with a "chrysoprase" stone surrounded by small satin glass stones.

A necklace set with presmolded stones, from Gablonz, possibly pre-World War I. This is a more naturalistic type of Gürtler-work, characteristic of the 19th century.

Germany and France was a very important step. During the transition period (roughly 1850-1870) this adaptation was accompanied by a repressing of local designs and traditions — and the pride in them. Indeed, some Gablonz Gürtler went so far as to denigrate their own pressed elements as being "primitive."[8]

In certain ways, the participation of the Gürtler and other Gablonz craftsmen at the Vienna World Fair in 1873 marks their official entrance into the world market of costume jewelry. Several generations of craftmen in many fields had had the time to perfect their skills. Members of all the crafts had improved, from the engravers and metalworkers to the painters, enamellers and electroplaters. These last were of particular importance, because the finish of most products depended on the electroplaters' skills; since 1850, electroplating had been used for coating non-precious metals.

Moreover, through the years the network of Gablonz specialists had learned how to cooperate perfectly. Early Gürtler had to manufacture every element by themselves or buy it from abroad. Now there was a diverse community of metalworkers, with whom the Gürtlers cooperated. Thus the Gürtler were able to concentrate on the design task.

The machinery for stamping and cutting high-quality elements was far too expensive for every single Gürtler shop to afford. In response to this financial impediment, some workshops had sprung up equipped with modern machinery where small Gürtler shops could have elements pressed from their own stamp patterns. This system allowed stamped elements to be ordered by them, as long as they could provide the necessary stamp.

For a great many of the 142 Gürtler with area workshops in 1856, however, even the financing of a specially-designed stamp was too expensive. Until the 1870s, these makers had no choice but to buy their elements from factories in France or Germany. By 1876, though, the number of independant Gürtler workshops had nearly doubled, prompting Gablonz Gürtler Emilian Posselt (1841-1918) to start the first *estamperie* — a large factory for stamped elements . His example was followed by the Gürtler Josef Scheibler (1850-1924) and Anton Markovsky (1848-1904) in the 1880s and 1890s. The Josef Feix & Söhne stamping workshop also developed into an important Estamperie. Scheibler, Feix and Markovsky remained the best renowned factories until 1945, each offering 15 or 20 thousand different stamped elements to the Gürtler during the 1920s and 30s. In addition, there always existed a great number of smaller estamperies.

Backed by such competent, experienced suppliers, the Gürtler reached an international level of jewelry production in the 1880s. Their success was stabilized by a high degree of organization. The first association, formed in 1839, had been prohibited, though; Austrian legislation considered such guild-like organizations to be an impediment to progress. The decades to come, however, made it only too clear that without a certain regulatory body, the competition between workshops and trade houses would become destructive and no standards of quality could be upheld.

The Austrian legislation was finally changed in 1884, and the Gablonz Gürtler immediately entered into a cooperative, which focused on the welfare of its members, particularly their education. Through this cooperation, the long-term stability and growth of the industry was secured. To illustrate their growth, in the town of Gablonz there were

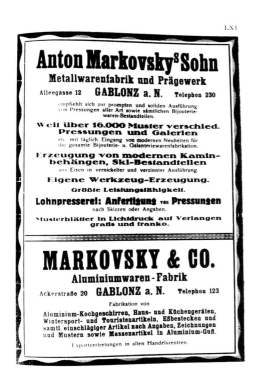

An advertisement from the Gablonz company of Anton Markovsky, 1924. This was one of the leading estamperies, supplying area Gürtlers with more than 16,000 different stamped elements.

256 master Gürtler, employing 561 Gürtler in 1884		
456	1042	1895
583	1881	1900
684	2592	1910
794	2391	1920
928	4379	1930

Three necklaces (including a festoon necklace) made from tombac; the upper two are gilded as well. Made in Gablonz, late 19th and early 20th centuries. While these pieces do not look particularly "Bohemian," they show one of many facets of the versatile industry.

A photograph of a lady in a festoon necklace. From Germany, 1890.

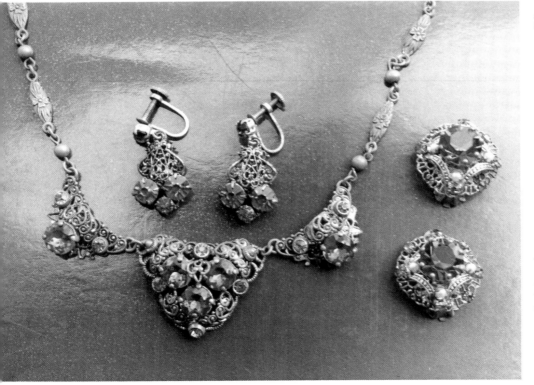

Necklace, earpendants and earclips set with blue stones. The necklace and earpendant are from Gablonz, 1930s; the earclips are from Neugablonz, 1970s. This is traditional Gürtler design and craftsmanship. The first stamped filigree had already been produced by the second half of the 19th century, but such old pieces in this form are rarely unearthed. Most that can be found date from the 1920s.

Three bracelets made in the traditional stamped filigree style. (left) Gablonz, 1930s; (middle) Enns/Austria, early 1950s; (right) Ernst Seidel, Warmensteinach, 1990. Pieces like these were once produced in great quantity in Gablonz. Gablonz Gürtler resumed the craft in various locations after World War II, but it is now rare to find craftsmen willing to invest the time and skill necessary to create such delicate bijouterie.

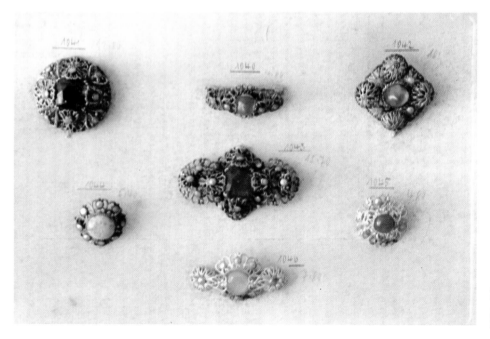

A sample card with "filigree" brooches from the 1950s, by Ernst Seidel, Warmensteinach. Early post-war pieces like these are often mistaken for much older work.

A photograph depicting various generations of the Seidel family in the early 20th century. As was often the case in Gablonz, family members worked in the same or related professions. In this photograph alone, there are three Gürtler. Standing at the right is Robert Seidel, metal-worker and father of Ernst Seidel. *(Courtesy of Ernst Seidel, Warmensteinach)*

A crucifix set with glass lapis cabochons, made by Ernst Seidel, Warmensteinach, 1990. This cross has been made in the best Gürtler tradition. It is apparent that it includes stamped elements in their entirety. To make it more difficult for competitors to copy their jewelry, Gürtlers cut such elements into various sub-elements, which they could then comnbine. This strategy was used particularly when a Gürtler used patterns from an "Estamperie," which other Gürtler were also free to use. The three-dimensional effect of the design pictured here and the high number of elements it incor-porates are noteworthy; they are signs of the highest level of Gürtler craftsmanship.

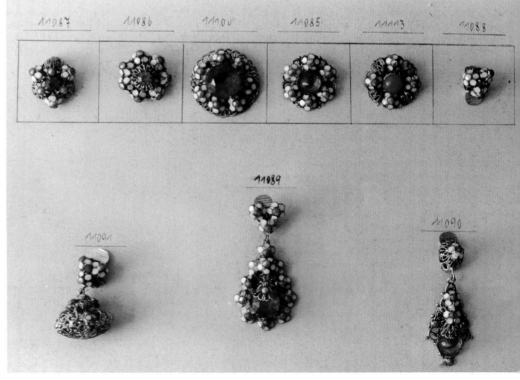

A sample card with earpendants and earclips made by Ernst Seidel, from the early 1950s. Again, the metal has suffered over the years.

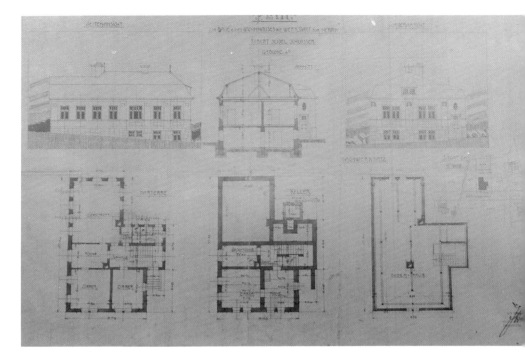

Robert Seidel (1884-1958) started his own metalworking business in 1910. In 1912, financed by the bank in Reichenberg, he built a house from these plans. Twice a year for thirty years, he put on his best clothes, walked 13 km to Reichenberg, made his loan payment and walked back again. In 1942, the loan was fully paid — and in 1945, everything was lost.

Aside from the craftsmen directly employed within the workshops, the Gürtler gave jobs to a significant number of cottage workers. In 1912, for example, 1100 cottage workers were employed, not counting their family members, who usually contributed as well.

The Gürtler workshops drew various metalworking industries to settle in Gablonz, but the workshops themselves remained small, family-run businesses. No matter how "cheap" the raw material may have been, every very good piece of Gürtler work was composed with imagination, craftsmanship and labor-intensive assembly-work. Only because of the high number of independent Gürtler workshops in the area were they able to produce such a high quality of jewelry in such great quantities that the idea of mass-production was categorically dismissed as unnecessary and unworthy.

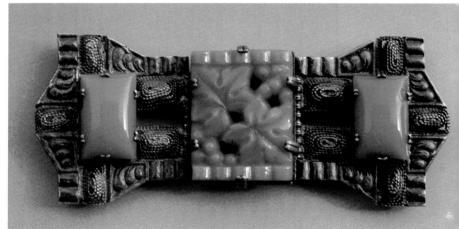

Two Gablonz brooches set with stones; (left) possibly pre-World War I, and (right) 1930s. On the bottom brooch, the natural motif has been reduced to nothing but foliage. Every stone is either carefully prong-set or bezel-set. Quality Gablonz Gürtler-work never inlcudes stones that are merely glued upon their bases.

Belt buckle with filigree elements, Gablonz. Pre-World War One.

Max and Norbert Neiger

The Neiger company was started around 1900 in the basement of the Neiger home, where 19-year-old Norbert was making his first jewelry. Even though he had successfully completed the Gablonz Technical School's bijouterie classes, these first pieces, crafted in his family's basement, were said to have been created with much regard for fashion (and less for quality). Thus they sold very well, and before World War I he enlarged his workshop, transferring it to the Berggasse.

At this stage, Norbert's younger brother Max joined him in the venture. Zitte reports that their early production line was one of long Egyptian-style necklaces, composed of silk-strung beads and a mummy-shaped pendant. Though these necklaces were expensive, they did very well on the market.[9] Their long strands, with beads spaced out along the silk cord, looked very much like molded glass bead necklaces made by French companies like Lalique in the 1920s.

The two Neiger brothers assumed different responsibilities within the company; Norbert ran the business, while Max headed the workshop and designed the jewelry. After World War I, the Neigers made Max's high-quality jewelry designs almost exclusively, though eventually they included items like scent bottles in their lines, decorated with stamped filigree and stones. (Bottles like these, which had been so important to the rise of the Gablonz industry, always remained a successfully selling product, and were produced by many makers.) The great demand, above all from American and English markets, caused the further expansion of the business. In 1926 the company moved into new premises in the Bebirgstrasse/Perlengasse. More than two dozen employees worked in the workshop, and more tasks were distributed to cottage workers.

The most important retailers and exporters bought from the Neigers. The high quality of the jewelry was matched by extremely effective presentations of each new collection. The former employee Ernst Seidel explained one such presentation for a 1935 design. A particularly elaborate collection, the pieces were geometrically-shaped bases (octagonal, oval or circular) gilded with exceeding care; they were finished with small center elements which were either enameled or gilded in a different shade. The central elements were impressed with patterns, sometimes floral, and eventually were set with stones (though no filigree was ever used). This collection was also made with a chromium-plated finish. To present this line (*Linie* was the Gablonz term for a collection with common design features), 150 of the brooches were arranged in the presentation room, hidden under a cloth. When all the important clients had assembled in the room, the cloth was suddenly whisked away. The full splendor of the collection, in 150-fold repetition, was exposed to each buyer's dazzled eyes.

An oblong flower brooch, by Neiger, Gablonz, 1930s. Similar flower brooches have survived changes in fashion since the late 19th century. This Neiger brooch is particularly fine, with excellent gilding.

A photograph of Norbert Neiger, his brother and partner Max Neiger, and their employees in Gablonz, circa 1925. *(Courtesy of Ernst Seidel, Warmensteinach)*

New collections like this one were generally conceived with a delicate balance between the Gürtler's own free artistic imagination and a creative adaptation to the requests of customers. No matter how imaginative Max Neiger was, since the Gablonzers were far from the world centers in which fashion success or failure was dictated, he always had to remember not to pioneer beyond the flexibility of the market. Max worked as well as possible within those restrictions. His own creations were daring enough to eventually inspire other makers in Gablonz and and even abroad — but for the most part he adapted to the wishes of his American clients. They came to Gablonz after passing through Paris, bringing with them the latest novelty jewelry, and asked him to create new lines to match those trends.

The Neigers did not stamp their own elements, but bought them from estamperies like Scheibler. To a certain extent, this gave other makers the chance to participate in the commercial success of the Neiger designs, since they had access to the same stamped elements. Generally, though, the jewelry that was "inspired" by Neiger designs did not equal the Neiger products in craftsmanship.

Even though all the high-quality makers in Gablonz had to tolerate such questionable competition, there were some legal means to impede outright copying. Thus, when a former employee of the Neigers started his own Gürtler workshop in the 1920s and tried to sell imitations of items from his old employers' shop, the Neigers were able to take the necessary steps to stop him. His entire production was confiscated.

The Neigers were considered among the most desirable employers in Gablonz. One former employee reports that of 34 employees at one point, 16 were Gürtlers. During the Great Depression, he wrote, no one was "made redundant." In the very worst period, "we just had to stop working and were not anymore paid. But soon, new orders came in again and we started working again."[10]

In 1938, this part of Bohemia was taken as part of the German Reich. The Neigers, who were Jewish, escaped with some of their employees into the adjacent Czech part of Bohemia where they continued to work on a small scale. Later they were arrested in Prague, and in 1942 they were killed in Auschwitz.

Brooch and pendant set with coral-colored cabochons, Gablonz, 1930s. The pendant is a genuine Neiger piece, while the brooch is most likely a copy of the Neiger design by another maker.

Three brooches in different styles of Gürtlerwork by Neiger, Gablonz, 1930s. In each season, the Neigers surprised their clients with new and imaginative collections. *(Courtesy of the Museum Warmensteinach)*

Pendant and brooch from Gablonz, 1930s. The pendant is an original Neiger piece, while the brooch was clearly "inspired" by Neiger. Since every collection of the Neiger company was a success, other makers frequently took their cue from Neiger designs. Most of the "copy" jewelry, however, cannot rival the Neiger's level of quality. Here, the Neiger pendant is carefully and characteristically gilded by the Jantsch company; the shade is exceptionally fine, and a

combination of a matte finish and a polished border adds lovely detail. The painting was done by the painter Svoboda according to a special technique: after the application, the paint was removed while still wet. Thus it remained only in the recesses, and the beholder has only the impression of a faint shade. The simple brooch at the left was painted in the standard way, though the paint has largely worn away.

An enameled pendant set with electroplated glass "marcasites," from Gablonz, 1930s. This pendant was not made by Neiger, though the manufacturer did have access to the stamped elements from the same Scheibler estamperie that Neiger used. This pendant is assembled with excellent craftsmanship from many separate elements.

The backs of the two Neiger pendants. The Neigers intended their bijouterie to look as good on the back as it did on the front. The smaller pendant in particular shows how well they succeeded.

The backs of three pendants (the preceeding one, and two from the Industry chapter) made in the 1930s. Gürtler-work's quality can be easily checked by looking at the backs of the pieces. The more care given to the backs, the higher the quality. In these cases, the makers covered the back sides with several stamped elements.

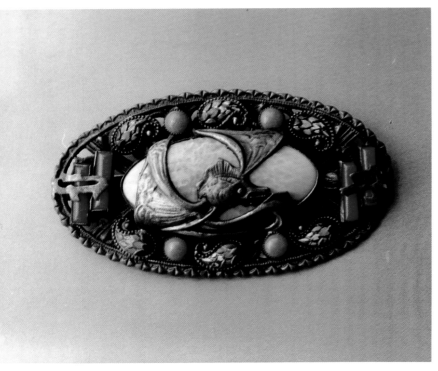

An oval brooch in a Chinese style, posssibly by
Neiger, 1930s.

A rectangular brooch in a Chinese style, possibly by Neiger, Gablonz, 1930s.

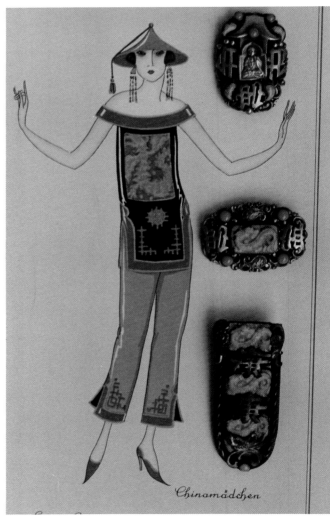

Chinamädchen

Two clips and a brooch in a Chinese style, by
Neiger, Gablonz, 1930s.

This large circular brooch in a Chinese design, possibly by Neiger, Gablonz, 1930s. The design is fine, but there is very little Gürtler-craft involved.

Brooch and bracelet decorated in Egyptian and Chinese styles by Neiger, Gablonz, 1920s/1930s. Exotic designs enjoyed a resurgence in popularity in the 1920s. The Neiger interpretation of these themes was particularly imaginative, and Max Neiger became a trendsetter among the Gablonz Gürtler.

Two brooches in Chinese style, from Gablonz, 1930s. The oblong brooch is by Neiger; the oval brooch may also be from this maker.

Two well-designed stamped filigree clips composed of a high number of elements and set with stones, from Gablonz, 1920s.

A photograph of a lady wearing a "filigree" brooch, Germany, circa 1880.

A particularly well-designed "filigree" brooch set with white stones, from Gablonz, 1920s. It is assembled from a very large number of separate, finely stamped elements. The central stone is made from frosted glass, molded with a radiating pattern.

A pendant set with a large molded stone, further decorated with stamped filigree, from Gablonz, 1920s. The filigree is of the same excellent quality as that on the brooch; it is likely that the elements came from the same estamperie.

A brooch set with especially fine rose-colored stones, from Gablonz, 1930s. The brooch is made from a solid element, upon which is attached (but not soldered) a rather crude filigree element. It is a well-designed piece, but required very little Gürtler craftsmanship.

A silver belt buckle transformed into a brooch, set with glass stones. From Northern Germany, mid-19th century. In the late 18th and early 19th centuries, such traditional jewelry was an important source of inspiration for the Gablonz Gürtler. Indeed, there were some Gürtler who continued to make real filigree pieces rather than adopt the use of stamped filigree entirely.

Brooch and clasp set with blue stones, Gablonz, 1930s. the brooch is assembled from various elements (though not a particularly large quantity); the clasp consists of a single element, to which has been added only the painted flowers. This is attractive but simple Gürtler-work.

The reverse side of the brooch and clasp, revealing the small number of separate elements.

A patterned filigree wire like those that served
as elements in some types of filigree bijouterie.
(Courtesy of the Museum Neugablonz)

A different type of filigree element, assembled
with labor-intensive handwork. *(Courtesy of the
Museum Neugablonz)*

Photograph of the Gürtler Hermann Hawel (d. 1991), the craftsman responsible for the filigree pictured here. *(Courtesy of the Museum Neugablonz)*

Filigree elements assembled into a final pattern. *(Courtesy of the Museum Neugablonz)*

Brooch and earpendants in filigree-work, by Franz Zasche (1839-1915) of Gablonz, possibly before 1870. This piece is not representative of the high craftsmanship and artistry that Franz Zasche eventually achieved. An imaginative Gürtler and an active participant in Gablonz society, his main concern was education; he was a strong proponent of opening a Technical School in Gablonz. He participated in the 1878 Paris World Fair, displaying a large selection of jewelry boxes, ear pendants, colliers and bracelets.

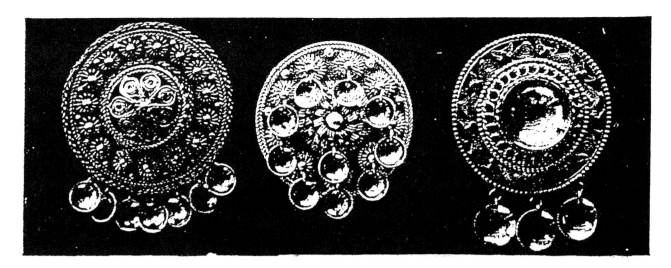

Illustration of filigree bijouterie made by Julius Zasche, Gablonz, 1888. This particular pattern was inspired by Norwegian filigree-work. Julius and Franz Zasche were contemporaries, but worked in completely independent workshops.

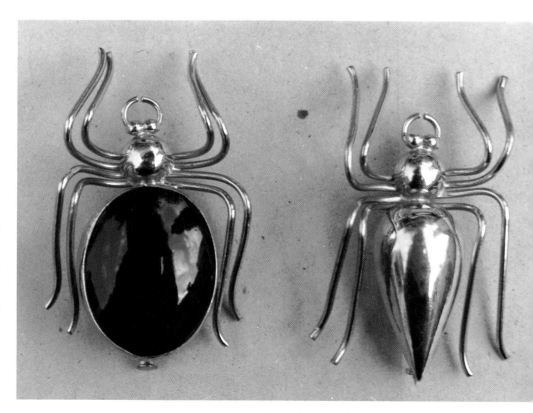

Advertisement for the company of Franz Ortelt, Gablonz, 1912. Ortelt specialized in filigree-work, and is considered to have been one of the best in the craft.

Two spider brooches by Franz Ortelt, Gablonz, 1920s/1930s.

Goldplated pendant and chromium-plated clip, from Gablonz, 1920s; possibly by Neiger. Elaborate Gürtler-work with stamped filigree decorations on the front and back. The filigree is enhanced with black paint. Even the small stones are not merely pressmolded, but cut on all facets.

Oval brooch set with cabochons, Gablonz, 1920s. This pattern was inspired by jewelry of the Wiener Werkstätte.

This chromium-plated bangle bracelet from Gablonz, 1920s, matches the pendant and the clip in the preceding picture. This piece of the set also features high-quality electroplating by the Jantsch company, combining a narrow polished border with a matte-finished center.

Brooch set with blue stones, Neiger, Gablonz, 1930s.

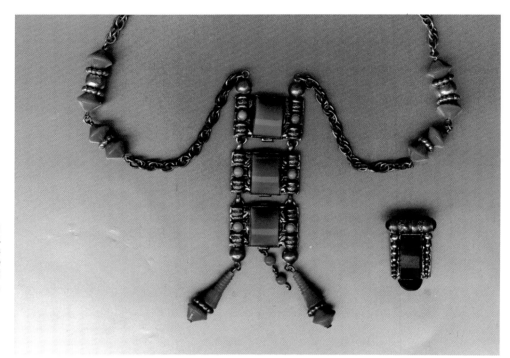

A necklace and a clip set with blue stones, from Gablonz, 1930s. These two pieces represent a very successful line from the '30s, which was characterized by stamped elements that are plain in comparison to stamped filigree, and opaque stones in classical colors like lapis, chrysoprase and carnelian.

A necklace and clip set with green stones, from Gablonz, 1930s. The Art Deco design is similar to that on the last necklace and clip.

Brooch set with two cabochons, Gablonz, 1920s. A Gablonz variation of the Austrian and German hewelry design, including embossed metal and spiraling wires. One brooch of this design line is included in the collection of the Museum Neugablonz.

A silver pendant decorated with three beads, from Gablonz, early 20th century.

Art Deco necklace and clip, set with coral-colored beads and stones, Gablonz, 1930s.

A brooch made of gilded silver and set with glass stones, by Siegfried Scharf, Gablonz, 1920s. *(Collection of Dr. G. Zasche, Neugablonz)*

A silver ring set with a glass cameo, accompanied by two pressmolded cameos, from Gablonz, 1920s. The two cameos are similar to that in the ring. They are molded in one piece from ivory-colored glass, and then enhanced with paint. *(Ring from the collection of Dr. G. Zasche, Neugablonz)*

"Real" Jewelry

Most bijouterie in Gablonz was made with non-precious metals, either silvered or gilded. But the handling of silver (the dominant Gablonz Gürtler metal in the 18th century) and even of gold never ceased completely in the area. Goldsmiths and silversmiths remained active in Gablonz, and some Gürtler as well did some silver work in addition to their usual work with non-precious metals. The link to old Gürtler traditions of the 17th and 18th centuries were restored in 1914, when the making of silver jewelry was reinstated in the regulations of the Gürtler cooperation.

In the directory of 1894, there are five makers working exclusively in gold and silver bijouterie. In the 1920s, 27 makers in and around Gablonz offered "*echte Bijouteriewaren,*" i.e. jewelry made from silver and gold. These included Rudolf Karneth (1877-1946), known for his enamelled silver butterflies, and Max Woperschalek (1871-1939), who began in the 1920s to concentrate on perfecting "Simili-Bijouterie." Simili-Bijouterie was made mainly from silver, mounted with the finest strass; it was intentionally designed to look like real jewelry. Heinrich Brditschka (b. 1886) created a great deal of marcasite jewelry in these years.

Photograph of a lady wearing a butterfly brooch, Germany, 1890.

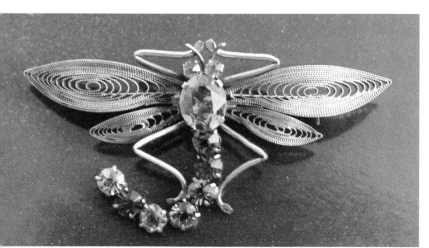

Spider brooch set with strass, Gablonz, 1930s.
(Collection of Dr. G. Zasche, Neugablonz)

Filigree dragonfly brooch set with stones, Gablonz, 1920s, probably by Franz Ortelt.

Spider brooch set with strass, 1930s.
Spider brooch set with blue stones, Gablonz, 1920s.
Spider brooch set with red stones, by "Spider Ettel," Neugablonz.

A butterfly brooch of enameled silver by Fritz Zasche, Gablonz, 1920s. Jewelry made of enameled silver was one of the greatest Gablonz success stories between the 1890s and the 1920s. *(Collection of Dr. Gertrud Zasche, Neugablonz)*

Two butterfly brooches set with multicolored stones, from Gablonz, early 20th century. The upper butterfly has movable wings and can be clipped onto the dress. This type of fixing was introduced in 1890 by Adolf Heidrich in Gablonz. Note that on both butterflies, every little stone is carefully prong-set, even though the bottom pin is only 2.5 cm in diameter.

Two butterfly brooches; (above) Gablonz, early 20th century, and (below) Otto Müller KG, Kaufbeuren, 1970s. The Müllers were renowned Gürtler for generations in Gablonz. The butterfly survived all changes in fashion, adopting many different forms. These included the classical butterfly (like the Weiss piece in the next picture) and the modern butterfly (like the Müller piece).

Two butterfly brooches set with stones; (above), Gablonz, 1920s, and (below) Weiss, USA, uncertain period.

Two butterfly brooches, Gablonz, early 20th century. Both butterflies are attractive, but of simple quality. Each stone is nonetheless prong-set.

Butterfly clasp, Gablonz, first third of the 20th century. This clasp catches the eye, but is rather low-quality. The stones are merely glued upon the wings.

Two butterfly brooches and an insect clip, from Gablonz, 1920s/1930s. The insect and the left butterfly were made with labor-intensive genuine filigree-work, while the right butterfly has elements of stamped filigree for its wings. Only very careful scrutiny can reveal this difference between the two butterflies; they are equally attractive.

Natural Materials

Up to the last third of the 19th century, the elements of Gablonz jewelry were primarily made of either glass or metal. This selection was considerably enlarged in the late 19th century to include various modern materials as well as some newly considered but very traditional materials.

One leading manufacturer in this field was Johann Schowanek (1868-1934). In 1896 he had founded a factory in Dessendorf to manufacture wooden articles, and in 1904 was induced by Gablonz exporters to start producing wooden beads. Wooden beads were light in weight, a great advantage for jewelry makers. Other manufacturers had already ventured in this production direction, competing with large beads made, for example, from natural jet. However, they were never able to color and polish them in such a way that they could stay attractive for a long period of time.

The Schowanek company took up the production of wooden beads and the making of celluloid and galalith beads simultaneously. They researched extensively the problems of coloring and polishing. In 1908 they founded a new company, "Johann Schowanek," in Albrechtsdorf — just in time to fully participated in the 1909 surge in demand for black wooden beads. Because their beads were of very high quality, the company became a leading supplier of such beads, and in 1914 was able to expand to 500 employees.

The post-World War I period saw the introduction of entirely new types of wooden beads created by the Schowanek workshops, including "enameled" wooden beads. These attractive beads facilitated an important rise in the production of beaded bags for export, mainly to the United States. In the early 1930s, the company ran in three shifts to satisfy the demand for such beads. They contracted with fourteen bag manufacturers, ensuring work for thousands of bead-making and handbag-making cottage workers in North Bohemia. In 1934, the company expanded to a thousand employees.

After the expropriation and the expulsion, a new Schowanek company was founded in 1949 in Bad Reichenhall to continue the family tradition.

Three brooches composed by cottage workers from Schowanek beads. Made in Gablonz, 1920s and 1930s. The background shows the wooden toys traditionally made in the adjacent Erzgebirge.

The company of Johann Schowanek in Albrechtsdorf.

Lady wearing a necklace strung with black wooden beads, Germany, 1909.

Two watch-chains made of black wooden beads, Gablonz, early 20th century.

Lady wearing a watch-chain composed of black wooden beads, Germany, 1914

Necklace composed of hand-painted wooden beads, Gablonz, 1930s.

Necklace and purse made of wooden beads, from Gablonz, 1930s. The beads are a standard Schowanek product. *(Courtesy of the Museum Warmensteinach)*

Lady wearing a bag beaded with large wooden beads, Germany, 1919.

Ballottini Beads

As early as the beginning of the 19th century, craftsmen were giving laquered wooden articles a satiny sheen by gluing crushed crystal on their surfaces.[1] In the late 19th and early 20th centuries, this type of ornamentation underwent an important revival: instead of ornamenting wooden articles, however, the craftsmen began decorating blown glass. Moreover, instead of using crushed crystal and broken glass for the ornament, they used "ballottini" — tiny glass balls — produced by manufacturers such as Breit in Wiesenthal. Ballottini were mainly used for technical purposes to render surfaces reflective, but since at least the 1920s the Gablonz jewelry-makers used them to decorated wooden beads.

Four necklaces strung with Ballottini beads; Gablonz, 1920s, and Neugablonz, 1950s.

Cobalt blue vase with "Coralene" ornamentation, Germany, late 19th/early 20th century. "Coralene" is the American term for this type of ballottini decoration.

Close-up of the post-war ballottini necklace; this one still shows a pulled pattern, but most ballottini beads from the revived Neugablonz industry were simply monochromatic.

Five strands of ballottini beads from Gablonz, 1920s. Most Gablonz ballottini beads show this pulled pattern.

Three vases with marbled decoration, Germany and North Bohemia, first third of the 20th century. Pulled decoration like this was fashionable during the 1920s.

Handcarved beads and baubles

Jewelry made from ivory, bone, mother-of-pearl and tortoiseshell was not a very broad production line of the Gablonz industry, but it did maintain a discreet, uninterupted presence from the early 19th century on. Some companies that made their fortunes working with synthetic materials also gave time and attention to natural materials. Franz Ulbrich's company mass-produced plastic jewelry and beads, but also created a small amount of bijouterie handcarved from natural materials such as ivory, mother-of-pearl and tortoiseshell. Ulbrich had recruited craftsmen from the Bohemian Forest and from Vienna to ensure that this facet of his Gablonz company would succeed. From ivory, these craftsmen carved flowers (including roses) and small animals. From mother-of-pearl and tortoiseshell (as well as from ivory) they carved high-quality beads for necklaces. Aside from this one important company, about two dozen other makers in the 1920s in the Gablonz area offered buttons and bijouterie made from mother-of-pearl or including it.

A pair of studs shaped like beer glasses, from Gablonz, late 19th century. The glass parts of the *Seidel* ("beer glasses" of this particular shape) are made from mother-of-pearl.

Photograph of a lady wearing a carved ivory brooch, Germany, 1888.

Three brooches carved from bone and ivory, Isergebirge/ Riesengebirge, late 19th century. These items were brought home as souvenirs.

Necklace including mother-of-pearl rings, from Gablonz, around 1920. This long necklace (130 cm) includes blue-tinted mother-of-pearl rings and some unusual pressmolded glass elements.

A mother-of-pearl brooch and a belt buckle in the shape of a horseshoe. From Gablonz, late 19th century.

Three clips made from mother-of-pearl, Gablonz, 1920s.

Bone Carving

The carving of bone had its roots in the Bohemian forest. When business for this craft slowed in the early 20th century, manufacturers from the Gablonz area attracted a great number of bone-carvers to their towns. These craftsmen adapted their talents to carve high-quality hand-made items from artifical materials. One such manufacturer was Franz Ulbrich, who started to employ many of these carvers after World War I. On a smaller scale, this company produced hand-carved items from other natural materials as well.

Carved bone brooch painted with dark and light green, Gablonz, 1920s. Such items of natural materials were the forerunners of the carved or molded Art Deco plastic jewelry—like the necklace show at the right!

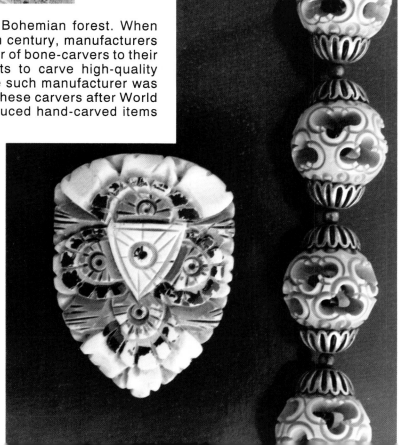

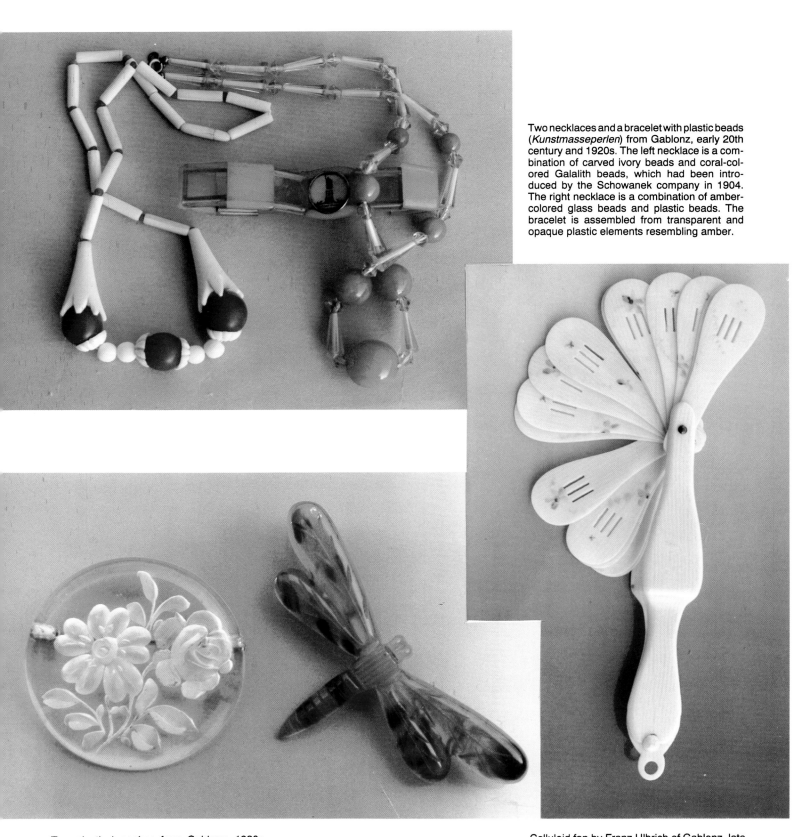

Two necklaces and a bracelet with plastic beads (*Kunstmasseperlen*) from Gablonz, early 20th century and 1920s. The left necklace is a combination of carved ivory beads and coral-colored Galalith beads, which had been introduced by the Schowanek company in 1904. The right necklace is a combination of amber-colored glass beads and plastic beads. The bracelet is assembled from transparent and opaque plastic elements resembling amber.

Two plastic brooches from Gablonz, 1920s. The circular brooch is decorated with intaglio machine-cut flowers. The "tortoise shell" insect has hand-carved decorations.

Celluloid fan by Franz Ulbrich of Gablonz, late 19th century. In this era, celluloid was predominantly used as a substitute for ivory and tortoise shell.

Synthetic Materials

One new field that the ever-expanding Gablonz industry embraced with great daring and enthusiasm was the manufacture of jewelry and other items from synthetic materials. In Vienna during the 1870s, the Gürtler Franz Ulbrich (1856-1929) grew familiar with celluloid, one of the first synthetics in common usage. Back in Gablonz in 1878, he introduced this exciting and versatile material to the craftsmen and industrialists, beginning yet another branch of Bohemian bijouterie.

The early days of celluloid crafting were filled with labor-intensive and time-consuming experimentation; celluloid was like nothing the Gablonzers had ever worked with before. It was delivered by foreign producers in large blocks, which were impossible to handle effectively with the methods and machinery to which the craftsmen were accustomed. Nonetheless, Ulbrich soon managed to start producing bangle bracelets and hairpins decorated with celluloid ornaments.

When the appropriate cutting machines were developed, the possibilities Gablonz craftsmen discovered were almost endless. Celluloid crafted in Gablonz for the "exotic" trade was made primarily into bangles, amulets, scepters and beads. For the "fashionable" trade it was shaped into hair combs, hatpins, buttons, studs, beads, toys and many other utilitarian objects.

Celluloid foil was worked into artificial flowers which were a great success on the market for many years. In 1894 Ulbrich introduced "coral" beads made of celluloid, and then similarly-made "amber" beads. The latter were to become a specialty of the company, produced in a large selection of sizes, ranging in diameter from a few millimeters up to ten centimeters!

Franz Ulbrich was a true pioneer in celluloid beadmaking, and thanks to him Gablonz became a world-renowned center for the production of celluloid beads. Up to 1914, almost every country in the world was supplied with celluloid articles from Gablonz. Moreover, Ulbrich supplied celluloid manufacturers in France, England and Germany with a great deal of valuable information to help them modify and improve the raw material of synthetic products.

The pre-World War I period had already seen other types of plastics which could readily lend themselves to jewelry-making, including Galalith and Bakelite. The designation "plastic" is used here as a general term for many synthetic materials, which until the 1930s could be divided into two major categories, based upon their chemical characteristics. The first are modified *natural materials*, such as celluloid and Galalith, which can be shaped by using a number of different methods. This type of plastic has been in use since the 1870s. The second type, in use only since 1909, are *thermosetting plastics*, which can be shaped only as they cool. Thermosetting plastics include Bakelite and Pollopas.

Before World War One, Gablonz had adopted the plastics that had been presented to them, including celluloid, Bakelite and Galalith. The post-war erea saw the development of an overwhelmingly broad selection of modified natural materials and thermosetting plastics. These new products immediately provided a true challenge to innovative and adventurous manufacturers like Franz Ulbrich. Between 1918 and 1938 his company experiemnted with almost every synthetic material which came onto the market.

Bangle bracelet made of ivory-colored celluloid with strass ornamentation, from Gablonz, late 19th/early 20th century.

Around the turn of the century, Ulbrich's company employed about a hundred workers. During boom times this number rose to as many as 130. In later years his sons Max (1889-1938) and Walter Ulbrich continued the family business, enjoying particular success with jewelry combining Gürtler metalwork and plastics.

Another important manufacturer of plastic articles was Carl Gewis (1867-1932). Beginning in 1900, he produced jewelry made of both celluloid and Galalith, employing up to 300 workers. Eventually the company restricted their production exclusively to technical products.

During the 1920s, the Gablonz area counted about forty craftsmen and manufacturers who produced jewelry that either included some plastic parts or was made entirely from plastic.

Fashion advertisement, spring 1925.

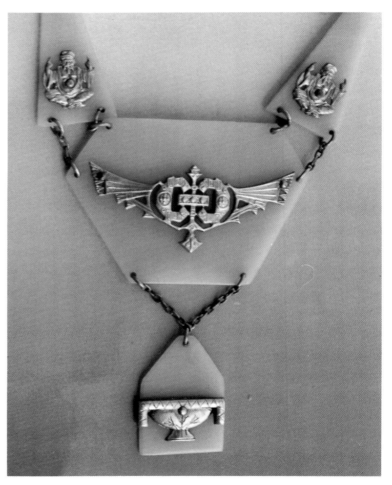

Long plastic necklace simulating horn, ornamented with metal. Gablonz, 1920s.

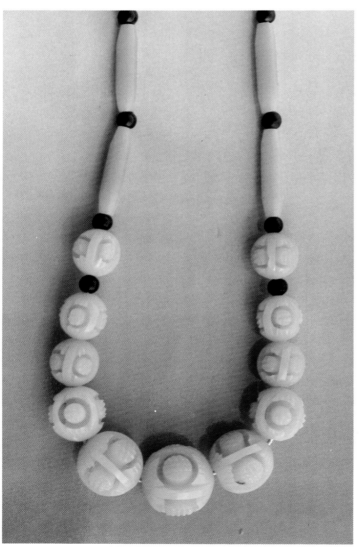

Plastic necklace including machine-carved beads, from Gablonz, late 1920s/1930s.

Two long necklaces composed of thin plastic elements from Gablonz, 1920s. The left necklace is decorated with a spider; it might have been made by the Gürtler Josef Ettel, who specialized in making flies and spiders (he was even given the nickname "Spider-Ettel").[1]

Necklace including carved plastic beads, glass beads and spacers set with strass. From Gablonz, late 1920s/1930s.

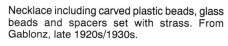

Long plastic necklace simulating ivory, including lampworked satin glass beads, Gablonz, 1920s. The insect on this necklace was most likely made by the Ortelt company.

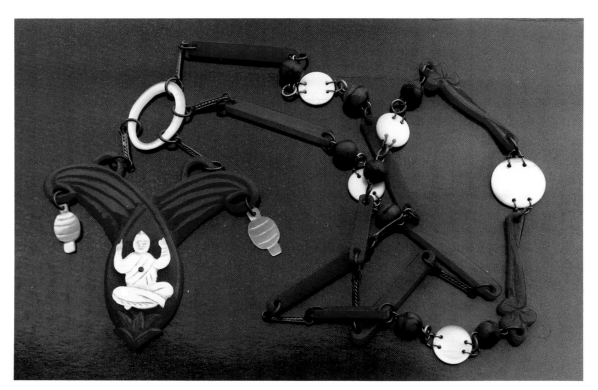

Long necklace composed of red plastic elements, Galalith beads and mother-of-pearl elements, from Gablonz, circa 1920. The elements are hand-carved.

Two Art Deco necklaces, Gablonz, 1930s. This style of necklace is generally attributed only to German makers. The design was certainly inspired by the trends in German arts and crafts, which were rejecting the traditional jewelry goal of looking "precious." The new design styles integrated modern mass-produced materials, and accepted undisguised technical production methods. Both of these necklaces are composed of metallic elements; the one on the right incorporates black and ivory plastic elements, while the one on the left features black and blue glass beads.

The Trading Companies

The making and trading of Bohemian glass articles was first centered in the area of Haida and Steinschönau, about 60 km west of Gablonz. Documents dating from the 17th century provide information about the trading network that started there and extended across all of Europe. The glass merchant Georg Franz Kreybich (1662 - c. 1736) left records of his travels, which led him to England and Sweden as well as to southern Italy and Turkey. In 1685/86 he was accompanied by Kaspar Hänisch from the Isermountains.* Johann Josef Kittel (1650-?) from Reichenberg/Gablonz also cooperated with Kreybich.**

In the first half of the 18th century, this trade had grown into such dimensions that it required new structures to support it. Between 1740 and 1750 a hundred export companies (*Glashandelscompagnien*) were founded, with affiliates in sixty cities of Europe, America and the Middle East (*Vorderasien*). In those years a growing number of merchants also settled in the Isermountains, in Liebenau, Kukan, Marschowitz, Morchenstern, Wiesenthal, Gablonz and the Kamnitzvalley. Those merchants were generally glass-*makers* as well. The versatile ones extended their travels ever further into Europe, visiting important trading cities and making contact with experienced exporters who could market the Bohemian Isermountain goods even further out into the world. They learned about trends and fashions in the great capitals, and brought this knowledge back to Gablonz with them.

The ever-growing demand for Bohemian glass beginning in the 18th century prompted the rise of a new class of glass merchants. The industry needed (and found) merchants familiar with the needs of the European and overseas fashion markets which were so far from the remote area of Gablonz. Different parts of the international market sought different modes of glass decoration, which the isolated Bohemian glass-makers could only keep up with through the travelling, worldly merchants. Within each individual foreign region, quickly changing fashions required immediate responses from the jewelry manufacturers; Gablonz needed to arrive at new patterns and new products to meet their customers' new styles.

The experienced merchants from glass-making and glass-refining families reshaped production structures to suit these challenging ranges and purposes, keeping in mind that the industry's foreign expansion would require great quantities of goods produced at ever-decreasing costs. To achieve these two goals, this new generation of businessmen took raw glass and undecorated items from the Gablonz glassworks, and themselves distributed it to the ever-growing number of specialized glass-refiners for the labor-intensive and variable work of finishing—including cutting, engraving, enameling and painting. Since the hundreds of competing refiners were mostly cottage workers or small family-run workshops, they had to be extremely malleable about setting prices for their work, and were often driven to desperation by the low payments they were forced to accept. Thus the glass merchants were able to influence not only the modes of decoration, but also the output quantity and the final prices of goods for eventual export.

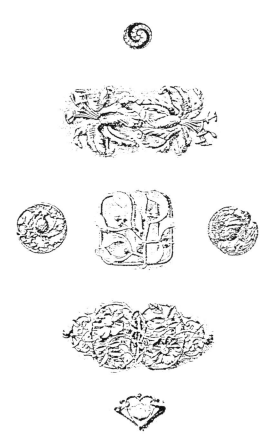

Art Nouveau jewelry made by Mahla in Gablonz, presented at the 1900 Paris World Fair.

* Presumably, Kreybich's companion was the Kaspar Hänisch who owned the Friedrichswald glassworks from the 1650s until 1689. Another Kaspar Hänisch was brother to Gottfried Hänisch, who took possession of that glassworks in 1695.

** Johann Josef Kittel was the glass-master at the Falkenau glassworks in the early 18th century; he produced a particularly well-regarded, high-quality Bohemian crystal. His grandson, Johann Josef Kittel, owned the Friedrichswald glassworks from 1752 until 1769.

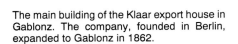
Iridized ink bottle and paperweight by E. Dressler, Gablonz/Berlin, late 19th century.

Aside from the Gablonz merchants who marketed primarily blown glass—such as Schwan or Johann Christian Weiss (?-1841)—a group of merchants arose in the first years of the 19th century who had already established themselves as stone merchants. These enterprising businessmen included Kaspar Wander, the last owner of the famous Grünwald glassworks, Wenzel Hübner, and Franz and Josef Dressler. Like Joachim Fischer, the Dressler brothers were the first real wholesalers of the area. In the 1820s and 1830s, there were a growing number of merchants who could already compete on the international market, including the companies of Josef Pfeiffer (Gablonz), Heinrich Göble (Gablonz), Karl Josef Zenkner (Josefsthal), Ferdinand Unger (Liebenau) and Blaschka & Söhne (Liebenau). During these early years Liebenau offered better transport facilities, and thus many exporters remained there.

The choice of articles which the Gablonz merchants offered got very favorable reviews: "the sample cards of some of the companies," commented one critic, "show a choice of several hundred different pearls [blown beads] and corals [massive beads], cross pendants and heart pendants, ear pendants, luster pendants...the companies represent a unique industry."[2] Statements like this indicate that in the 1830s, Gablonz was already growing into its role of leadership in the bijouterie community.

During the 1850s, the merchants from Gablonz were well-appreciated in jewelry-makers' most important forums. Anton Ignaz Seidel had shown "not less than 640 different samples in strass" at the 1855 Paris World Fair, wrote one impressed reviewer.[3] On the same occasion, the Prediger company from Tannwald had shown other articles, such as buttons, pearls, bracelets, rings, lockets and pendants for candelabra. The great selection of "Bohemian diamonds" offered at the Paris event indicates that in those years the fashionable French and English "paste" jewelry had already come to rely on the strass elements from Gablonz. In later years there are even more explicit statements that the jewelry industries in England, France, Germany and the United States were the main buyers of stones from Gablonz.[4]

The Gablonz exporters represented their industry with another large selection of goods at the World Fair in New York in 1856. Josef Keil, for one, showed rosaries and "Rocailles," in addition to the type of articles listed above from the Paris World Fair.[5]

In 1860 we can find 161 merchants in the Gablonz area, 31 of whom were based in Gablonz proper. Those merchants originated from old local families with even stronger traditions of making glass and bijouterie than of trading it.

The sudden expansion of the industry between 1860 and 1870 made a major change necessary, however. This decade attracted important outside exporters

The main building of the Klaar export house in Gablonz. The company, founded in Berlin, expanded to Gablonz in 1862.

from Germany to Gablonz; these merchants dealt directly with every corner of the earth, all the while maintaining a staff of carefully trained employees in Gablonz. Unlike the traditional exporters, they never intended to expand their concerns into manufacturing as well. They depended on the internal and external trading networks which had been established by the old companies, and used many local maker/merchants as intermediaries between their companies and the thousands of independent manufacturers in the area.

The dominance of the export houses drove the makers into even greater anonymity. A chronicler made notes about the Gablonz 1878 Paris World Fair displays, mentioning "Schindler & Veit, Gablonz, much renowned for their beads, buttons and bijouterie," and "Eduard Dressler, Gablonz, [who] exposed Bohemian diamonds, paperweights, and similar items."[6] In reality, these companies had neither designed nor manufactured the items which bore their names in the exhibits; they merely distributed and marketed them. These two particular merchants were among the best-known Gablonz exporters, keeping company with other firms like Jacob & Heinrich Mahla, Wilhelm Klaar and A. Sachse.

These experienced exporters were the final element in the highly sophisticated network of manufacturing and marketing Gablonz bijouterie. They contributed decisively to the success of the entire region and its industry.

Nothing better illustrates the world leadership of Gablonz's glass jewelry and bijouterie since the end of the 19th century than a look into an 1888 French directory of the glass industry.[7] Of the 64 companies listed as suppliers of glass bijouterie, 54 are based in the Gablonz. This, however, may not be apparent, since the villages in the few square kilometers that make up the Gablonz area are all listed under their individual names, including Albrechtsdorf, Johannesberg, Josefsthal, Grünwald, Maxdorf, Morchenstern, Neudorf, Tannwald and Wiesenthal.

Artificial pearls — generally associated with places like Paris or Vienna — are noted in the directory as being manufactured by 4 companies in England, 15 in France, 18 in Germany, 29 in Vienna, 36 in Italy and 60 in the Gablonz area! In the directory can also be counted the suppliers of small articles of glass: 2 in the United States, 4 in England, 9 in Germany, 28 in Italy, and 140 from the area of Gablonz! This directory does not just show how tremendously prolific the Gablonz industry was; we can also tell what unparalleled significance it had in the world market. We can conclude from this French publication that the French retailers dealing with similar "*objets de fantaisie*" and with fashionable jewelry were very good customers of the craftsmen and merchants of Gablonz.

Advertisement for the renowned Jäger company, Gablonz, 1926. The company marketed stones as well as bijouterie.

European makers and exporters of glass jewelry, listed in a French directory from 1888.

BIJOUTERIE EN VERRE (FABR. DE)

GLASS JEWELLERY — GLASSCHMUCK — BISUTERIA DE CRISTAL — BIGIOTTERIA

(Voir aussi *Verroterie*)

Allemagne

Greiner & Co, Bischoffsgrün (Bayern).
Greiner (Louis), Igelshieb b. Steinach.
Schmidt (Max), Bayreuth (Bayern).

Angleterre

Northwood (J. & J.), Wordsley (Stourbridge).

Autriche

Benkert (J. C.), Wiesenthal.

Bergmann (Anton), Gablonz (Böhmen).
Bergmann (Franz), Gablonz a/N.
Dressler (Edouard), Gablonz a/N.
Dubsky (Max), Leipa (Böhmen).
Endler (Heinrich), Gablonz a/N.
Eulefeld (Gustav), Gablonz a/N.
*Feix (Gebrüder), Albrechtsdorf, b. Morchenstern. (V. l'ann. à *Verrerie*.)
Fischer (Anton), Gablonz a/N.
Fischer (Joh.), VII Lindeng 24, Wien.
Goldzieher (A.), Bäckerstr., 4, Wien.

Grossmann (Joh.), Morchenstern.
Günther (Friedr.), Steinschönau.
Hagemann & Fritz Meyer, Gablonz.
Hesse (M. & E.), Gablonz a/N.
Heyda (Carl J.), Gablonz a/N.
Hittmann (Anton) Sohn, Wiesenthal.
Hoffmann (Carl) & Sohn, Josephsthal b. Maxdorf (Böhmen).
Hollabetz (Franz), Gablonz a/N.
Hübner (Adolf), Gablonz a/N.
Hübner (Ad.) & Söhne, Gablonz a/N.
Hübner (F. J.), Morchenstern.
Huyer (Clemens), Gablonz a/N.
Kahl (Ferd.), Gablonz a/N.
Kisch (J. M.), Gablonz a/N.
Kittel (J. F.), Kukan, b. Gablonz.
Klaar (Wilhelm), Gablonz a/N.
Kramer & Löbl, Gablonz a/N.
Kratzer (Gebrüder), Grünwald, b. Gablonz a/N.
Lederer (K.), Gablonz a/N.
Löhnert & Heinrich, Steinschönau.
Löwenthal & Hesse, Gablonz a/N.
Mendel (Daniel), Gablonz a/N.
Meyer (Desiderius), Gablonz.
Möller (Josef), Schlag, b. Gablonz a/N.
Müller (Emil), Gablonz.
Pam (Jos.), Gablonz.

Patzelt (A.), Josefsthal, b. Ob. Plan.
Pfeiffer (Jos.) & C°, Gablonz.
Philipp (Oscar), Gablonz a/N.
Pospischil (V. J.), Wiesenthal, b. Reichenberg (Böhmen).
Preisler (Anton), Josefsthal, b. Maxdorf.
Rahm (Erich), Wiesenthal.
Riedel (Jos.), Polaun (Böhmen).
Rössler (Anton), Gablonz.
Rössler (Wilh.), Gablonz a/N.
Sarder (Theod.) & C°, Gablonz.
Schmelkes & Kretsch, Bäckerstr., 4, Wien.
Schoeler (Jos.), Morchenstern.
Schuster (C. W.), Gablonz a/N.
Schuster (Moritz Th.), Gablonz a/N.
Schwarz (Ed.), Gablonz a/N.
Spitzer (S.) & C°, Gablonz.
Strauss (Gust.) & Co, Gablonz a/N.
Umann (Joh.), Tiefenbach (Böhmen).
Veit (Carl), Gablonz a/N.
Wawra (Joh.) & Söhne, Morchenstern.
Wünsch (J. F.), Gablonz a/N.
Zenker (Gebr.), Josephsthal, b. Oberplan (Böhmen).
*Zingel (Johann), Gablonz a. N. (Voir l'annonce à *Verrerie*).

No. 785.
Matted Finish, Pearl Center.
$1 25

No. 786.
Finish, Polished B
$1 25

No. 788.
Matted Finish.
$0 75

No 789.
Real Onyx and Gold, Matte
$11 00

Two brooches of typical jet bijouterie, Gablonz, late 19th century. In the background is a page from the 1896 Marshall Field catalog. Marshall Field purchased a large amount of its merchandise from Gablonz.

Portrait of Hugo Jäckel

The company of Josef Pfeiffer

The glass merchant Josef Pfeiffer is mentioned for the first time in 1820 when he founded a company with Karl Josef Riedel. Riedel (1767 - 1843) had inherited the Christiansthal glassworks from his father in 1794. Unlike his older brother, who owned the prosperous Neuwiese glassworks, Karl Josef Riedel fell prey to the economically difficult years at the beginning of the 19th century. These financial woes may have been the reason he entered a contract with Josef Pfeiffer, a successful merchant from Gablonz; they might also have been the reason Pfeiffer dissolved the contract soon afterwards.

In 1829, the company Josef Pfeiffer & Co. took part in the exhibition of Bohemian products in Prague, showing composition, artificial gemstones, faceted beads and pendants.[8] To judge by the quantity of the products offered, the company was not yet as important as Göble's company, for example, which presented ten times as many items. But Pfeiffer may just have been offering a partial selection; his production was geared mainly for foreign markets, while the collection shown in Prague was clearly aimed at the home and European markets.

Pfeiffer kept a close watch on the glass industry in Murano and Venice, and in the 1840s tried to start production in Gablonz of various items previously made exclusively by the Venetians. He recruited beadmakers and glass-makers from Murano and Venice, and in 1847 began producing Rocailles, lampworked beads, paperweights and adventurine.[9] Furthermore, Pfeiffer was most likely one of the first merchants to compete with the Venetians in the African trade.

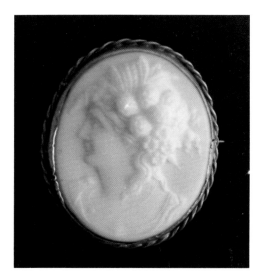

Cameo brooch from Gablonz. Late 19th/early 20th century.

Swivel brooch with an impressive gold mount. The cameo is identical to the one shown to the left; the mount is most likely from England, late 19th century.

The Pfeiffer company remained a leading exporter in the following decades as well. It was among the 44 companies (of 200 exporters in existence in the area) that did the preliminary work to represent Gablonz at the Vienna World Fair in 1873. Among the various articles chosen for this exhibition was a large piece of aventurine made either by the Pfeiffer company or by the Jäckel company; the Riedel glassworks at Klein-Iser did not begin to produce aventurine until 1879. Virtually every glassworks in France and Germany had tried in vain to compete with Murano (the city that founded this sparkling glass) in the production of aventurine for the international market. It is quite remarkable that in the 1870s Gablonz could already boast of three different manufacturers of this glass.

Despite the many economic crises in the Gablonz industry, the Pfeiffer company remained a successful exporter until the very end of the industry. During the late 19th century and the first half of the 20th century it was clear that they restricted their focus primarily to the European and North American bijouterie market; nonetheless the selection they offered remained very broad.

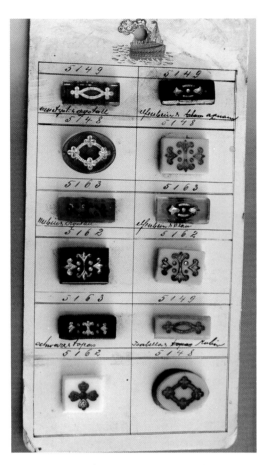

Sample card with stones to be mounted into watch chains, by Frit Sch & Co., Gablonz, 1910.

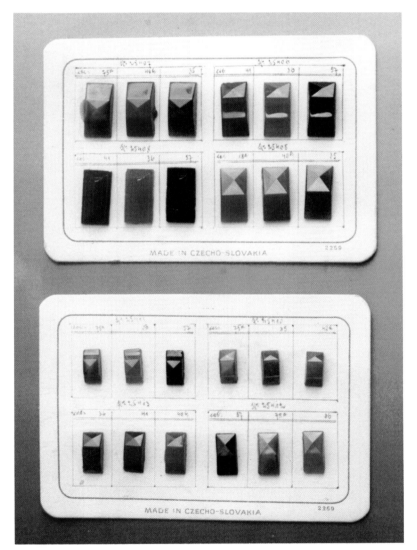

Sample cards of Franz Kuhn's company, from Gablonz, late 1920s. The company, founded in the early 20th century, specialized in glass stones.

This made of decoration is extremely labor-intensive. The stones and the tiny inlays silvered, assembled and, finally, cut and polished.

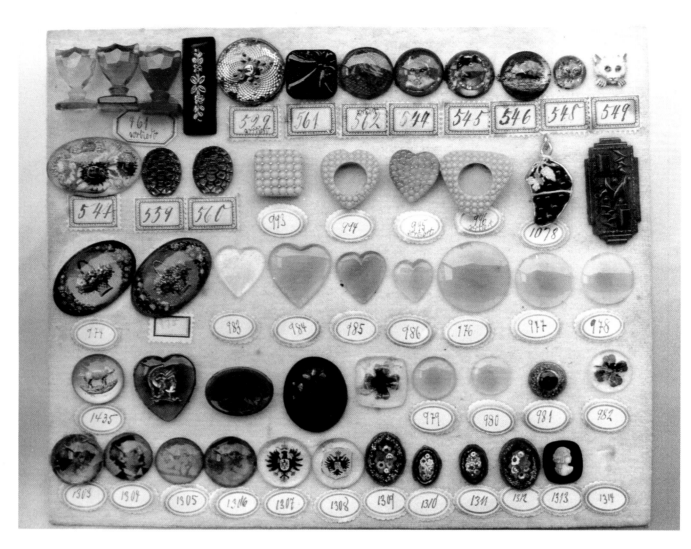

A sample card with various glass stones from Gablonz, early 20th century.

Close-up of the sample card, showing turquoise- and coral-colored stones. Such stones, called "turquoise berries," were ornamented with gilded dots, and were the specialty of the Kukan glass-maker Emil Ulbrich.

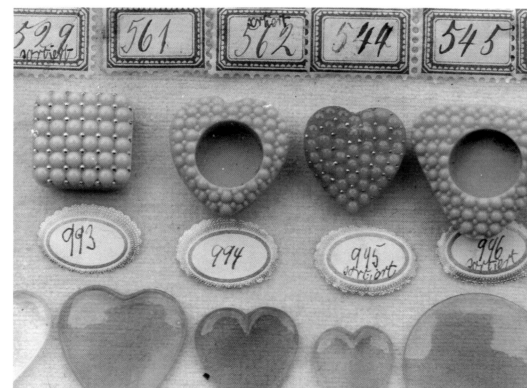

Two brooches including mosaic stones identical to those found on the sample card. The gold mounts are of uncertain origin; the lower brooch was assembled from two ear-pendants.

Cameo and intaglio stone as shown on the sample card, Gablonz, early 20th century.

Golden brooch set with a "turquoise berry." The mount is probably English, early 20th century.

A brooch including an engraved and gilded stone, and an unmounted stone. From Gablonz, early 20th century. Another virtually identical oblong stone can be found on the previously pictured sample card.

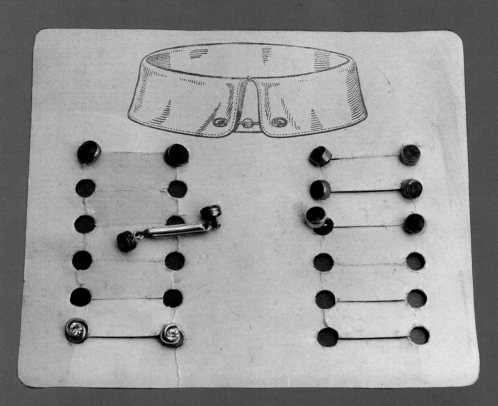

A sample card with collar studs from Gablonz/
Oberstein, late 1920s.

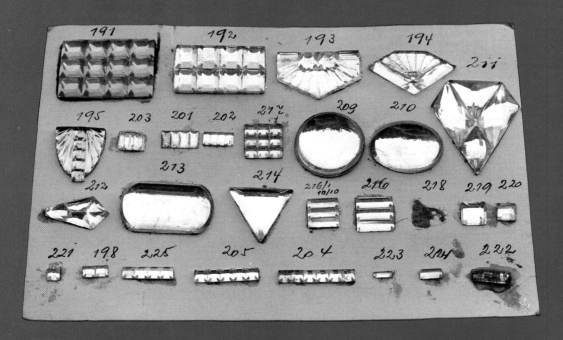

A sample card including pressmolded and silvered stones in fancy shapes. From Gablonz,
1920s/1930s. The card was sent by the exporter Löwy to the Bengel company.

Bangles for Export

Around 1850, the Christiansthal glassworks began to produce large tubes, with diameters of up to 4 cm. These were cut into rings, ornately decorated by glass-refiners, and sold as napkin holders.

These tubes were soon to be adapted to an entirely new use. The Gablonzers had long since established trading links with India, and between 1870 and 1880 they became aware that Indians used glass bangles extensively for ornament. Their demand had been covered predominantly by Chinese makers, but when some pioneering manufacturers from the Isergebirge tried to enter this new market, they were immediately very successful. The early bangles were elaborately decorated, cut and enameled, much as the napkin rings had been, but the makers soon realized that their highly sophisticated bangles were not required for the Indian market. They standardized their production to a pressmolded "threefold"* bangle, which was then refined by cutting and enamelling. The production soon split into the making of "common bangles" which were not refined by cutting at all, and the making of various bangles with more elaborate designs. The makers in the upper Neisse valley created different types of overlay bangles, including striped ones, and the Johannesberg makers created a variety of "fancy-mirror-bangles".** Lampworked bangles, made from patterned canes, were first created around 1908. The procedure of making those wound bangles was considerably simplified after World War I: the reheated cane was wound in a 4 mm thread around a metallic core. the spiral was cut lengthwise and the open ends were later joined together by cottage workers. Starting in 1928, the Riedel company supplied machine-wound spirals, which were further refined by cutting, gilding or enameling.

The bangle industry, exporting first to India and then to the Middle East as well, was started by a small number of companies, including the Emanuel Hüttmann company in Antoniwald, and the Emil Müller and Carl Walldorf companies in Gablonz. The immediate success of this new branch of the Gablonz industry caused countless others to join the promising bangle business. No other item of the industry required so much glass as the bangles, and soon all the glassworks in the Isermountains were producing bangles. The makers in Gablonz even had to involve outside glassworks in Bohemia and in Moravia to supply them with bangle-glass.

Competition between the bangle-exporters soon grew out of control. Various efforts were made to keep the market from being ruined by excessive manufacturing and drastic price-cutting. The "Gablonz Glassbangle Syndicate Ltd." was founded in 1904 and was joined by thirty-five companies. The syndicate brought prices and salaries to an acceptible level, and the entire industry prospered. But within three years the market was again ruined by newcomers, and in 1910 the syndicate was dissolved.

The early 20th century was the peak period in the bangle business. Shiploads of bangles were sent through Trieste to Bombay and Basra, and through Hamburg to Madras, Calcutta, Rangoon and, again, Basra. The steamer "Gablonz" was on its first journey in April, 1913, loaded with 6000 boxes, each filled with 200 dozen pairs of bangles—the standard contents of a bangle box—bound for Bombay. The yearly export before World War I amounted to 180,000-200,000 such boxes—i.e., 28,800,000 bangles!

* The rings got flat cuts (generally 12); two further rows of cuts were applied upon the ends of the slightly tilted rings. Thus they were decorated with a pattern of lozenges in the middle and triangles on both ends.

** The English terms "common bangles" and "fancy-mirror-glass bangles were in common use in Gablonz at this time.

BANGLES

The steamer *Gablonz*, which began transporting bangles from Trieste to Bombay in 1913. The ship was renamed *Tevere* in 1919, at the same time that the *Austrian Lloyd* became *Lloyd Triestino*.

Two filigree bangles and a gilded bangle from Gablonz, 1920s/1930s.

Three bangles with enameled decoration, Gablonz, 1920/1930s.

World War I brought the bangle business to an abrupt end, but the exporters resumed trade as soon as the war ended. Production of the high-quality "fancy-mirror-bangles" continued without major disturbances, though the out-of-hand production of the common bangles continually necessitated the formation of new syndicates to keep competition within bearable limits. The export of bangles never again reached the pre-war heights, but was limited to between 20,000 and 50,000 boxes annually. The "fancy-mirror-bangle" market remained more or less in the hands of the Gablonzers, though they lost part of the common bangle market to Japanese and Indian competitors. Moreover, their own troubles on the money market hurt the bangle industry; since prices of bangles were agreed upon in pounds sterling, the devaluation of that currency affected Gablonz's export business severely.

The outbreak of the Second World War ended the bangle business permanently.

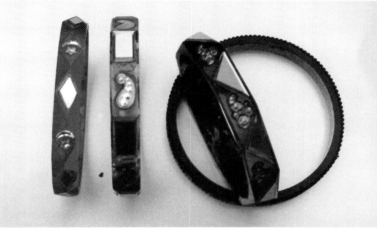

Four bangles with various applications, from Gablonz, early 20th century.

Four striped bangles, Gablonz, 1920/1930s.

A necklace with mirror applications, from Gablonz, 1920s. This attractive technique began in the early 19th century.

Three "fancy mirror" bangles from Gablonz, early 20th century.

Baubles, Buttons and Beads:
The Artistry

Glass has always been the dominant material in Gablonz bijouterie. While it was sometimes meant to serve as a surrogate for "the real thing," more frequently it was used to create jewelry items in genuinely new designs possible only in glass. Today, fashion jewelry with artifical glass stones posing as "real" gems has become the craze among collectors, while the beautiful pieces made by more innovative craftsmen are relatively neglected.

In this domain we can discover tremendously sophisticated modes of glass decoration, which appeared only much later in blown glass, and we can discern some very interesting types of glass, which remained exclusive to the bijouterie makers. Glass painting and enamel work, overlay and bi-colored glass, satin glass, saphiret glass, iris glass, spatters trailings, mosaics, jet, mosaics, and intricate pressmolding—all these methods drew upon the various fascinating qualities of glass, making each finished piece a work of art, unmistakably and undisguisedly *glass*.

One expert described the Gablonz bijouterie of the 1850s in this way: "The glass dominates. Those glass elements don't pretend to be something else, but proudly show their own specific characteristics. This tells clearly from what roots the bijouterie industry in Gablonz has grown. The metalwork does nothing but humbly frame the glass art."[1]

Painting and Enameling

Painting

From the very beginning of the Gablonz bijouterie industry, glass was enameled and painted. One of the earliest mentions of a glass-painter is of Franz Heidrich in 1761. The first half of the 19th century attracted many porcelain painters to the area, where for the most part they decorated pipeheads. In the 1870s, the expanding button industry began to require the skills of painters as well. For most years, little is recorded about the precise number of painters, but in 1938 the area could count 2000.

One renowned painter was Wilhelm Würfel. He was born in Haida, and after some wandering years settled as a master painter in Schlag. In 1890 he entered into a fruitful button-painting collaboration with the Gebrüder Feix company in Albrechtsdorf. Feix's buttons were anything but standard products, and they were delivered to the most elite fashion houses in Paris and New York. Their little works of art were produced not in hundreds or thousands but only by the dozen. For one series, Würfel was paid the extraordinary sum of 1.25 crowns per button.[1]

A button with a painted portrait. The mount is English; the painting is probably Gablonzer, from the mid 19th century.

A violet brooch from Gablonz, early 20th century. The brooch includes a crystal cabochon with a molded and painted intaglio on the back. The motif is backed by a mother-of-pearl plate.

Postcard with violets, Germany, 1918. In the early 20th century, Germany and Austria experienced a *Biedermeier* revival; people cherished these nostalgic flower motifs.

Two buttons with handpainted silver and gold decorations. From Gablonz, second half of the 19th century.

A painted brooch from Gablonz, 1930s. This type of painted work, intended to resemble enameling, was produced in abundance. This particular brooch, carefully crafted from ten separate elements, surpasses the usual simplistic quality of this jewelry.

Enameled brooch with flowers, Gablonz, early 1920s.

A pendant with enameled paint, from Gablonz, early 20th century.

A brooch in a "Mary Gregory" motif, from Gablonz, early 20th century. This enameled painting style was widespread in the Gablonz area, primarily for export to the USA and to England. It is found most frequently on blown glass, and only rarely on stones like this one intended for jewelry. (Courtesy of Andrew Lineham, London)

Enameling

The enameling of bijouterie became of central importance starting in the 1880s. The Viennese manufacturers had initiated this fashion (hence the tern "Viennese enamel") and the major exporters in Gablonz were obligated to include such jewelry into their collections to satisfy clients. The Technical School responded immediately to the new demand by starting classes in enameling in the mid-1880s, and the Gablonz craftsmen and students quickly became adept at the technique. Indeed, while the term "Viennese enamel" is standard in the United States, most "Viennese enamel" jewelry has come from Gablonz since the early 20th century.

Two special varieties of enamel made in Gablonz were called silver enamel and mosaic enamel. The silver enamel's background was heavily plated with silver, which was engraved with a delicate guilloché pattern. This pattern shone through the transparent enamel in a very attractive way. In mosaic enamel, the entire enameled surface was made up of tiny millefiori slices.

Between 1892 and 1900, the number of enamelers grew rapidly, rising in the best periods to about 120 masters enamelers. One of the first important masters in Gablonz was Franz Fleischmann, whose career started with a single stick-pin, enameled with a swallow against a white background on its circular top. Another renowned enameler was Rudolf Karneth (1877-1946). He began his career as a master engraver and not until 1904 started his enameling workshop. The demand for his jewelry was so overwhelming that he was forced continually to expand his workshop, finally employing as many as fifty workers. He made a great variety of articles, and was particularly well-known for his silver enamel and mosaic enamel.

The popularity of enameled jewelry came to a sudden end in 1929. Most enamel workshops in Gablonz had to turn to new tasks and new arts.

Iris belt buckle, Gablonz, turn of the century. An identical buckle enameled with slightly different shades is included in the collection of the Museum for Glass and Bijouterie in Jablonec.

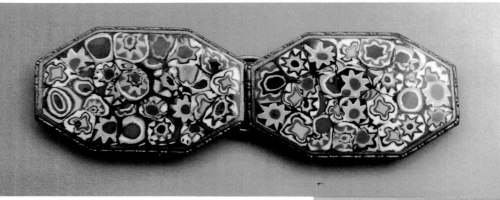

A clasp with mosaic enameling, from Gablonz, early 1920s.

Brooch and pendant with enameled frame, set with a satin glass cabochon. From Gablonz, early 20th century.

Two brooches in large enameled frames, set with satin glass cabochons. Gablonz, early 1920s.

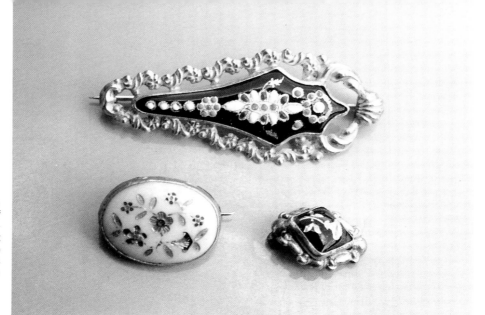

Two brooches and part of an ear-pendant with enamel decoration, from Germany, first half of the 19th century. The upper brooch was originally part of an ear-pendant. Merchants brought sample pieces of new fashionable jewelry to Gablonz, which the area's makers could use as inspiration to make similar stones for the foreign jewelry market.

A leather handbag decorated with an enameled plate, from Gablonz, first third of the 20th century.

Handbag with enameled frame, from Gablonz, early 20th century. The handbag is framed with fine Gürtler work, and is set with cut stones, pearls and enameled elements.

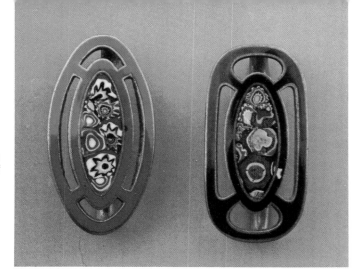

Two scarf-holders with mosaic enameling. From Gablonz, early 1920s. Possibly from Rudolf Karneth's workshop.

Three brooches with enameled stones from France and Gablonz, late 19th and early 20th centuries. This type of enameling was common practice in France, though Gablonz was quite active in it as well. The process reproduces enameling techniques from previous centuries.

Souvenir brooch depicting Dover Castle, made in Gablonz in the 1930s. Gablonz makers received special orders for novelty products like this from clients all over the world.

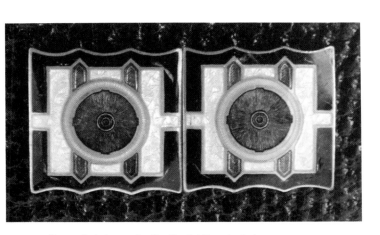

Enameled clasp reflecting the Art Deco taste for strong color contrast. From Gablonz, late 1920s.

Two blown pendants made of overlay glass. From Gablonz, early 20th century. The pendants are lined with gold and silver and are cut to reveal the lining. Pendants like these were mounted for ear-pendants.

Two silver gilt earrings set with ruby-flashed stones. The early 20th century Gablonz stones are carefluuy cut and backed with silver foil. At the left, a ruby-flashed paperweight from Bohemia, late 19th century.

Bi-colored vase from North Bohemia, early 20th century.

Two necklaces with bi-colored beads from Gablonz, 1920s and 1930s. These beads display three types of color combinations: yellow/green (uranium-colored glass) to rose (selenium-colored glass), blue to yellow, and blue to rose.

Overlay and bi-colored glass

Bohemian blown and cut overlay glass was a European craze, marketed as a novelty all over the continent beginning in the 1820s. Such compound glass, however, was far from "novel" to the Muranese and Bohemian beadmakers, who had been using the technique of combining two or more differently-colored glasses long before glass-blowers started. Still, the early 19th century popularity of blown and cut overlay glass inspired the Gablonzers to create new overlay designs for the bijouterie industry as well.

The bijouterie makers were also inspired by the glass-blowers in the creation of bi-colored glass, a type of glass that had been particularly well-appreciated from antiquity. The fascinating effect of changing shades within the glass can be achieved either through chemical processes, or through the simple physical combination of two different color glasses. For chemical techniques, glass-makers use or combine constituents which they have discovered will produce the desired bi-colored effect — uranium added to Bohemian potash-lime glass, for example. Another successful chemical method uses gold as its constituent. Physical combination of glasses is basically a simple overlay, but this fact is not apparent when the two colored glasses are transparent; they seem to mingle in the light, blending their shades in a lovely shimmer.

Glass-makers used yet another technique, striking, to achieve bi-colored glass. Striking is achieved by reheating glass to change its color; when only a part of a piece of glass is reheated, it produces two colors within the one piece.

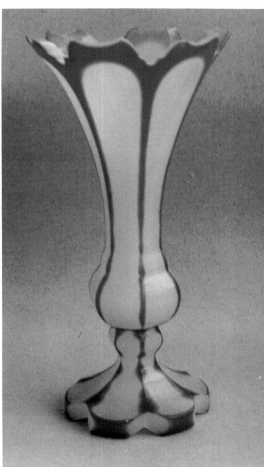

Cut overlay vase from North Bohemia, first half of the 19th century.

Four necklaces including bi-colored beads, from Gablonz, 1920s and 1930s. In these pieces the double color is achieved by combining blue and yellow canes of transparent glass.

Cut overlay elements for buttons, Gablonz, 1850s/1860s.

Brooch including a crystal and blue glass element engraved with flowers and backed by silver paint and plaster. The gilded mount is probably English; the glass is from Gablonz, early 20th century.

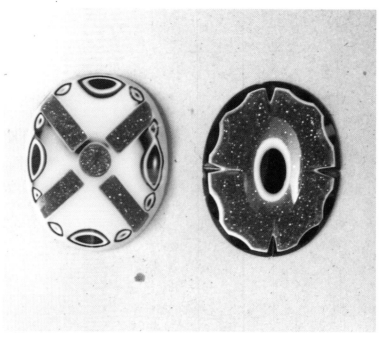

Two cut overlay elements from brooches, Gablonz, 19th century. The element at the right has a remarkable *5* layers: black, white, black, aventurine, white. A standard overlay combines only two or three layers; a multiple overlay like this one is a singular achievement.

Satin Glass

In the 19th century the composition makers in Gablonz created a variety of glass which they called *Seidenglas* (satin glass); its satin-like sheen was the result of combining opaque and transparent glass within one cane. It was also known as *Mondscheinglas*, literally, moonshine glass; a better translation would be "moon*stone* glass," however, since the white variety of the glass resembled natural moonstones. The glass canes were twisted, or impressed with patterns on the opaque part, producing very intriguing irregularities and reflections in the glass. No two pieces of satin glass were alike.

Starting in the late 19th century, satin glass was the most successful glass for the Gablonz bijouterie industry. Almost every significant glass or composition maker had developed its own specific (and patented) variety. The Brosche company held a patent for its variation around 1910, and the Eduard Redlhammer and Konrad Dressler companies each held a satin glass patent. The Riedel company also successfully produced its own type of satin glass.

Two enameled brooches set with yellow satin glass cabochons. From Gablonz, early 20th century. The yellow variety of satin glass is so well-made that it is frequently mistaken for amber.

Two brooches set with satin glass cabochons from Gablonz, late 19th/early 20th century. On both of these pressmolded stones, it is evident that the original glass cane was twisted before pressmolding.

A necklace with moss-green satin glass beads, from Gablonz, 1920/1930s. This necklace incorporated unusual and elaborate metal spacers set with small satin glass stones.

Two brooches including satin glass cabochons, from Gablonz, 1920s. The metal elements are enhanced with "cold enameling" — i.e., painting.

A silver brooch with a blue satin glass stone. From Gablonz, 1920s. *(Collection of Dr. G. Zasche, Neugablonz)*

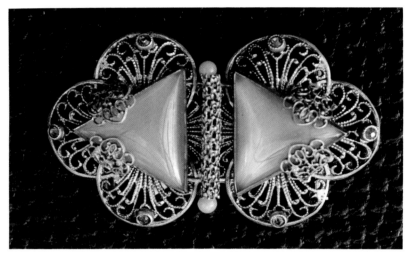

A clasp including rose satin glass cabochons. Gablonz, 1930s.

Brooch including satin glass cabochons, and a satin glass ring. Gablonz, 1920s.

An enameled pendant including a large cabochon molded with a star pattern, intended to resemble a natural star sapphire. From Gablonz, 1930s. This technique, in various colors, was extremely successful; it is still in production today.

Saphiret Glass

Though the original name, saphiret glass, has not survived the years, this was a very popular Gablonz bijouterie glass created in the 19th century. Its bi-colored appearance results from gold, which is added as an ingredient to a basic sapphire blue glass. In the second half of the 19th century, there are references to saphiret glass which fetched higher prices than gold-ruby.[1] It can be found in some of the finest Art Nouveau jewelry.

A brooch with a large saphiret cabochon, from Gablonz, first third of the 20th century

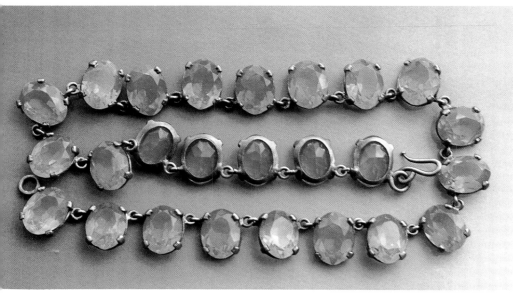

A necklace composed of faceted saphiret stones, Gablonz, 1930s. The fascinating dichroism of the saphiret glass — showing either a sparkling sapphire blue or an almost opaque brick red — is particularly visible in this picture.

A silver button transformed into a brooch and set with saphiret stones. From Gablonz, early 20th century.

Three pendants with saphiret stones and strass, Gablonz, early 20th century. The coronet settings, generally used for natural stones to ensure maximum light refraction from all sides, were probably acquired from abroad.

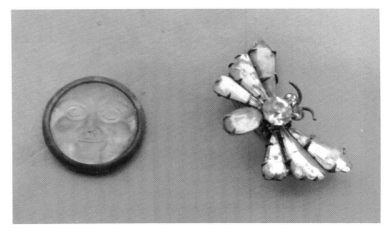

Three brooches including saphiret stones and strass, Gablonz, late 19th/early 20th century.

Two brooches with cut and frosted saphiret stones, from Gablonz, late 19th/early 20th century.

A button and a brooch with saphiret stones. From Gablonz, late 19th/early 20th century. The button is pressmolded with a face. The fly brooch has movable wings and can be clipped onto a dress. This type of fixing was introduced in 1890 by Adolf Heidrich.

Iris Glass

The use of natural rhinestones (Cailloux du Rhin) is recorded in Germany and France since at least the 17th century. This variety of quartz is also called either rainbow quartz or iris quartz because of the certain amount of of iridescence it shows due to its internal fracturing. It is found in the Alps and is brought down to the valleys by such rivers as the Rhine — hence the name *Rhine*stones.

Bohemian composition makers re-created this stone in glass during the late 19th century. Among the makers, the glass stones were called iris glass, though on the European market they were largely called simply "rhinestones." They were (and are) very popular, and can be found frequently set into very ornate silver jewelry.

A brooch showing a faceted "rhinestone" from Gablonz, late 19th/early 20th century. The background shows some natural tourmalines of the dichroic "watermelon" type, whose shadings correspond very closely to this creation by a Gablonz lampworker.

Four pendants with "rhinestones," from Gablonz and Germany, after World War I.

Three brooches including "rhinestones" and strass, from Gablonz, late 19th century. The old pre-World War I rhinestones have much stronger colors than the more recently crafted stones.

Three necklaces with "rhinestones," from Gablonz and Germany, after World War I.

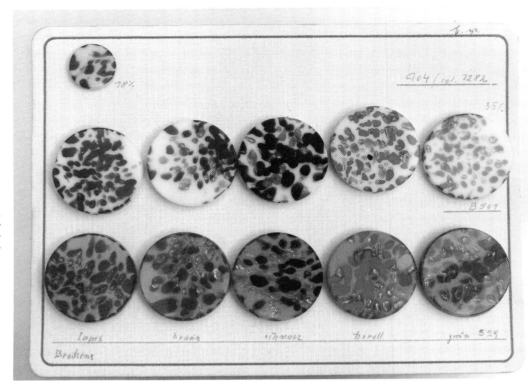

Sample card with flecked stones, by Wilhelm G. Wildner, 1973, Neugablonz. The tradition continues, as we still find black and white combinations, including aventurine spatters on alabaster buttons.

Brooch and clasp including fancy glass cabochons, from Gablonz, early 20th century (brooch) and 1930s (clasp). This sophisticated variety includes spatters and trailings encased between satin glass ands clear crystal. The making of such cabochons was very time-consuming.

A vase decorated with glass threads from north Bohemia, early 20th century. Such glass is known as "peloton" glass. The technique began to be used on blown glass around 1880.

Fancy Glass
Spatters, Trailings and foil inclusions

The early glass craftsmen's first concern was to re-create the sparkling colors of natural gemstones. Beginning in the last decades of the 19th century, however, they developed a growing tendency to create imaginative mulitcolored glass pieces, which bore only a roundabout resemblance to natural gemstones. Using such simple means as spatters, trailings and (silver) foil inclusions, the lampworkers achieved a never-ending range of fancy glass and composition.

Cut alabaster buttons decorated with black and aventurine spatters, from Gablonz, 19th century. The buttonmakers produced a great variety of rather large decorated alabaster buttons in this era, with black and white buttons a particular favorite.

A vase with spatter decoration from North Bohemia, 1930s. Such spatter designs in strong contrasting colors were very popular on blown glass during the Art Deco period.

A brooch including a black cabochon decorated with white and aventurine trailings, from Gablonz, late 19th/early 20th century. The Muranese bead-makers have been lampworking their beads with fancy trailings since at least the 16th century. Similar patterns were adopted by Gablonz lampworkers in the early 19th century.

"Opal" brooch and two "opals." The brooch is early 20th century, from Gablonz; the opal element is merely painted. The loose stones, however, are modern and include silver foil; made by Schuhmeier of Neugablonz.

Two brooches including stones with large flecks in contrasting colors, early 20th century. Stones from Gablonz, silver mounts from England (right) and France (left).

Vase with mica flecks, from North Bohemia, early 20th century. Mica glass like this became a favorite fancy glass in Victorian times.

Silver brooch including a large cabochon with mica flecks, from Gablonz, 1930s. (Collection of Dr. G. Zasche, Neugablonz).

Two necklaces including foiled beads and stones, from Gablonz, 1920s. The foil is always silver, though it is covered with different colors of crystal.

Late 19th century brooch including a large cabochon. The stone cabochon is pressmolded from opalescent glass with mica flecks, from Gablonz; the mount may also be from the region.

Necklace with foiled beads and stones, from Gabonz, 1920s. Such necklaces were a very successful design line.

Side view of the brooch. The elaborate border of the mount includes bats. This motif has been used frequently by Art Nouveau artists since the 1890s.

MÄRCHEN AUS TAUSENDUNDEINER NACHT
GEMÄLDE VON PROF. JULIUS DIEZ
AUS REPRO-KUNSTHAUS MÜNCHEN

Belt buckle and belt element using foiled stones, from Gablonz, early 20th century. This variety of foiled glass is very sophisticated and very labor-intensive. Most of the stones and beads created thus were mounted either into mounts of precious metal or into very fashionable costume settings of the Art Nouveau style.

Silver brooch including foiled stones. The stones are from Gablonz, early 20th century; the mount is possibly from England, also early 20th century.

Paperweight with mica flecks and millefiori, from North Bohemia, turn of the century and early 20th century. Glass incorporating mica was made in Thuringia, Silesia and Bohemia frequently, starting in the early 1870s. It became an international craze after being shown at the Paris World Fair in 1878.

Mosaic glass

A special type of mosaic jewelry had been introduced to the European market by Murano's Domenico Bussolin in the late 1830s. Johann Hübner, from Kukan, began his experiments with it in Gablonz during the 1840s. Hübner, the son of a glass-cutter, had of course received his primary training in his father's craft, but eventually made his mark in the area of lampworking and mosaics instead. The fact that Gablonz craftsmen, starting with Hübner, chose to take up production of the Bussolin mosaic line indicates that it must have enjoyed a great market success.

In Murano, Bussolin's technique was already well-rooted, but Hübner most likely had no basis from which to begin. As his granddaughter decribed it, he developed his own procedures "in a time-consuming trial-and-error method....He got the circular, oval or rectangular canes from the Harrach factory in Neuwelt. He glued short cuts of those canes according to prepared patterns upon a basis. The completed mosaic was covered with a layer of crystal and finally cut and polished."[1]

The mosaics were done in various sizes, to be set in studs, earrings, brooches and the covers of tobacco boxes. Once, the important manufacturer Josef Pfeiffer ordered an entire table top from Hübner. This masterpiece was surely meant for an exhibition.

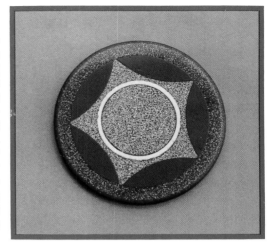

A mosaic element from Murano, circa 1840; possibly by Domenico Bussolin. This type of glass mosaic was used in various contexts, including as ornamentation of furniture. Bussolin was the first craftsman to create small elements suitable for jewelry-making.

A panel with mosaic elements made by Johann Hübner of Gablonz, 1840s-1870s. The panel was assembled in 1905 by Hübner's great-grandson, Josef Zeh. *(Courtesy of the Museum Neugablonz)*

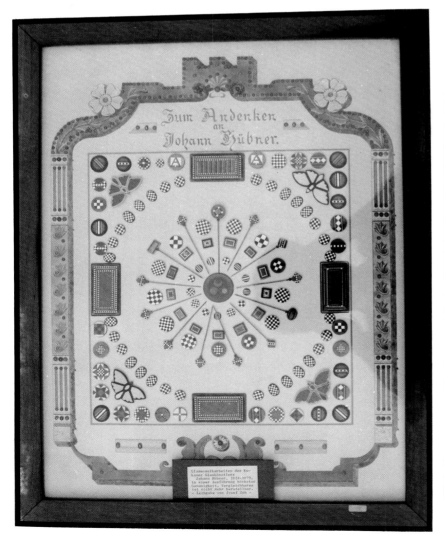

Hübner was extremely secretive about his work. He never hired any assistants, and even the members of his own family were not allowed to enter his workshop. His eight daughters could contribute only by helping him to cut and polish the mosaics.

A close-up of the panel. The design of the central mosaic reveals the influence of Bussolin's work. The small mosaics were mounted into buttons and studs.

Another close-up of the Hübner mosaic panel, showing some very elaborate rectangle mosaics. The elements were assembled upon overlay glass. Its border was cut round to reveal the various layers of glass.

Another close-up of the panel, showing more mosaics and a butterfly cut of overlay glass.

Jet Design

In the field of blown glass, the color black knew success only for very limited periods of time; however, since the 18th century black glass was consistently a very important part of the bijouterie industry in and around Gablonz.

The first truly sophisticated design line including black glass was created in the first half of the 19th century. Square elements with triple overlay (if not more) were decorated with fancy cutting. The cuts revealed the various glass layers, and the pieces were mounted into typically large "Biedermeier" brooches. Similar elements were also used for buttons.

The designers of this jewelry were well ahead of their time; black and white overlay glass like this turned up again almost a hundred years later, a much-demanded feature of Art Deco blown art glass. The mid-19th century black and white glass mosaic designs of Gablonzer Johannes Hübner were revived in Italian mosaics, and also among the Viennese Secessionists; designer Koloman Moser had quite a fancy for Hübner-esque checkerboard patterns.

A brooch including an overlay square, from Gablonz, circa 1840.

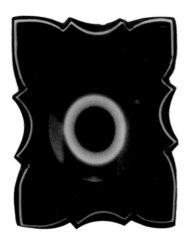
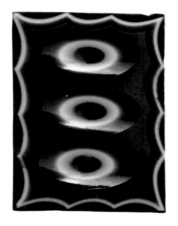

Two squares of overlay glass, composed of one white layer and two black layers. From Gablonz, first half of the 19th century. These squares were generally mounted onto brooches. *(Courtesy of the Museum Neugablonz)*

Hyalith bottles from the Silberberg glassworks in Bohemia, 1837. The glassworks of Count Bouquoi began producing blown glass in black in 1817; it remained fashionable for about 20 years. Since that era, though, blown glass of this color has never regained its popularity. *(Techincal Museum, Vienna)*

A lady in a dress with imaginative jet decoration.
Germany, 1890s.

A lady wearing a jacket elaborately decorated
with glass jet beads. Germany, 1860s.

Lady in a dress decorated with an abundant
supply of glass jet beads. Germany, late 19th
century.

The imaginative jet beading on dresses of the 19th century can also be counted among the genuinely original uses of the seemingly insignificant Gablonz black bead. These examples of black glass design were rarely executed by Gablonz makers, however; the black bead elements were manufactured in Gablonz, but the designs of bead-upon-cloth were patterned and executed elsewhere.

This does not mean that the Gablonz craftsmen did not find any outlet for their creativity and inventiveness through black jet, though.
Gablonzers created stupendous lines of glass jet bijouterie, which dominated the market in the late 19th and early 20th centuries. This jet bijouterie was composed of small glass elements attached (originally with glue) to metal bases. The earliest glass jet enjoyed its first success around 1850, but in Gablonz it most likely did not start until the end of that decade. The region's tax registers for 1856 do not include any "jet-gluers" (*Glaskitter*),[1] but by the early 1870s there are plenty of them, mainly in Gablonz, Neudorf, Wiesenthal and Morchenstern.

A brooch molded from black glass by Heinrich Hoffmann, Gablonz, circa 1910-1914. *(From the Lobmeyr collection, Vienna)*

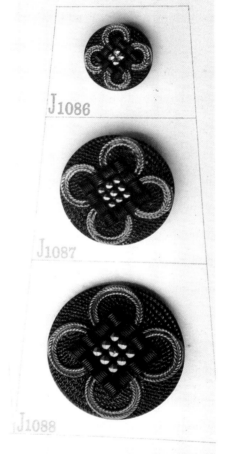

Black buttons pressmolded with an intricate pattern, further enhanced with a metallic coating. From Gablonz, 1889-90. During the second half of the 19th century, pressmolded buttons occupied a very special niche in the field of black glass design. *(Courtesy of the Museum Neugablonz)*

The first glass jet work was strongly inspired by the design of jewelry made from natural jet. The glass jet bijouterie of the later 19th century had freed itself from such precedent, however, and had developed its own design styles. From the very beginning, jet jewelry from Gablonz included not only flat and polished glass elements, like those found in French jet jewelry, but also pressmolded elements, at first only in semi-circular form, but soon afterwards in more complicated fancy shapes.

Because glued elements were so easily lost, in the 1870s makers introduced the riveted jet. In 1877 the Paris company Veit & Nelson took out a patent on a specific variety of riveted jet,[2] which the Feix company in Gablonz bought. This riveted jet was rather difficult to make, so the Gablonz makers simplified the technique: simply stated, the pressmolded elements were given metallic bases, and were then soldered onto the metalwork. One particular and widely-used variety was called "wire soldering" (*Drahtlötung*). In this method, craftsmen prepared a cast of the finished piece of jewelry, in which the glass elements could be arranged. Thus fixed in their proper places, they were soldered onto the wire. This procedure allowed the Gablonz artisans to construct extremely large and fragile jet ornaments.

Black buttons pressmolded with a fabric pattern, from Gablonz, 1889-90. *(Courtesy of the Museum Neugablonz)*

Jet bijouterie by Prediger of Morchenstern, early 20th century.

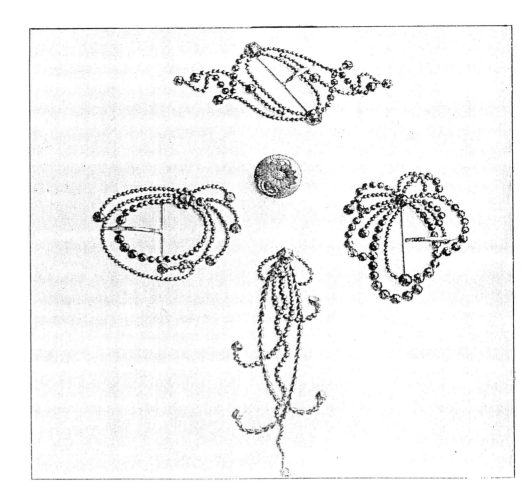

Mourning jewelry exported by the Mahla company from Gablonz, shown at the 1900 Paris World Fair.

Necklace with iridescent black beads, from Neugablonz, 1960s. Iridescent black beads were also tremendously successful as dress decoration during the last third of the 19th century.

Metallic Design

Luster and iridescence were the first important metallic decoration modes in the Gabonz industry. Another method, electroplating, was originally intended for the use of the Gürtlers. However, the glass decorators were also able to open new horizons of their craft with electroplating. Since Gablonz had an abundance of electroplating workshops, it was quite natural for Gablonz glass artists to start experimenting with this electro-chemical procedure.

Paul Weiskopf was among the first to recommend this treatment to decorate "brooches, buttons and beads,"[1] and he experimented extensively to find adequate solutions. Later, the company of Adolf Zasche became the leading manufacturer of electroplated glass, holding the title for several decades. They showed blown glass decorated this way at various important exhibitions.

This process became of central importance to the bead, button and bijouterie industry in Gablonz, and prompted the creation of entirely new designs. The success of this "Galvano-design" also prompted the extensive use of silver and gold for painting on glass.

Advertisement for the company of Adolf Zasche, Gablonz, 1924.

An illustration of Bohemian glass decorated by Adolf Zasche of Gablonz; these pieces were displayed at the 1900 Paris World Fair.

Vases decorated by Adolf Zasche, Gablonz, 1913.

A brooch set with a large stone molded in a marcasite pattern from Gablonz, early 20th century.

A brooch with electroplated glass marcasites, from Gablonz, early 20th century. Galvanized glass beads and stones were among the most successful production lines of this period.

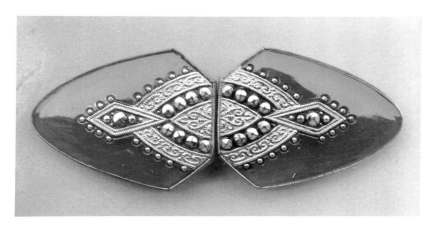

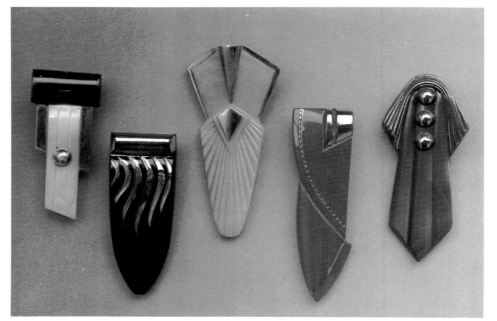

A clasp set with molded cabochons, from Gablonz, 1930s. The metallic mount was pressed with a pattern almost identical to that with which the glass carnelian from the previous picture was set.

A clasp set with carnelian-colored glass elements, from Gablonz, 1920s. The stones were molded with a pattern, and then were gilded to resemble a metallic application with marcasites.

Several clips with silver decoration, from Gablonz, 1920s/1930s. These pieces were mass-produced by the Gablonz industry in a staggering variety of designs.

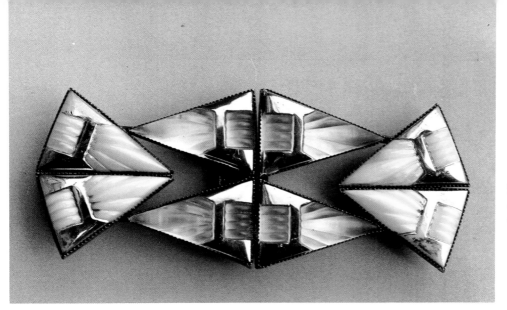

A clasp set with silvered stones molded of frosted crystal and yellow satin glass, from Gablonz, 1920s/1930s. A particularly well-balanced modern-looking design.

A clasp molded with a traditional pattern and electroplated with a bronze coating, from Gablonz, 1930s. Bronze coatings on beads and buttons were enormously successful on the market, starting in the last third of the 19th century.

Clasp molded of red glass and decorated with silver, from Gablonz, 1930s. This traditional piece is eyecatching because of its strong colors.

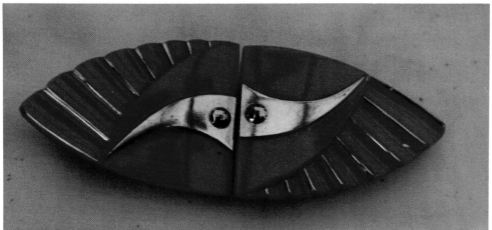

Sample card with red buttons by Hübner of Grenzendorf, 1935. In the 1930s, these type of buttons were considered standard and unremarkable; only now, decades later, can their strong design qualities be fully appreciated. *(Courtesy of the Museum Neugablonz)*

A clasp molded of red glass with a geometric pattern, Gablonz, 1930s.

A clasp molded of coral-colored glass painted with silver, from Gablonz, 1930s. A genuine Art Deco piece.

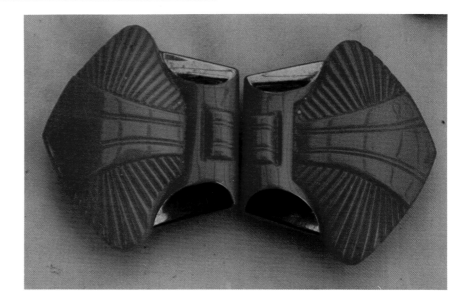

Pressmolded Design

In Gablonz, pressmolding was the most commonplace technique for crafting glass, but some of the designs at which the artisans arrived are so outstanding that they deserve a closer look–and full appreciation of their artistry.

As is the case with many of the fine products from Gablonz, most of these were created anonymously, and we will never know who designed the patterns, who engraved the molds, or who pressed and finished the glass. These imaginative pieces can only be attributed to the inspired air of genius that filled this town, this region and its residents.

One particular type of pressmolded glass to attain international recognition, however, can be linked to the names of Heinrich Hoffman and Henry G. Schlevogt. Hoffman was a well-known personality in the area, known by everyone as the *Kaiserliche Rat*– the Imperial Councilor. He was awarded this title by the Emperor Franz Josef I for his exceptional glass, specifically the glass eyes produced by his lampworkers. The Hoffman company had been founded in 1867 in Marschowitz by Heinrich's father Franz, and from the start they were known for the high quality of their beads and gemstones.

Around the turn of the century, Heinrich Hoffman began a Paris-based business, "*Henri Hoffman, fabrique de verrerie d'art.*" He made good use of the close connection between Paris, the center of fashion and art, and Gablonz, the center of high-caliber craftsmanship. His business was exceedingly fruitful, an inspiration for other makers in Gablonz.

In the late 1920s, Heinrich's daughter Charlotte married Henry G. Schlevogt. In Schlevogt, Heinrich found a congenial new partner, and the two began to work together. In 1934, Henry Schlevogt presented his "Ingrid" collection, named after his baby daughter, at the spring fair in Leipzig. The Ingrid collection was mainly made up of molded glass in the color termed "jade," a malachite shade of green. Some designs were linked to Hoffman's romantic sense of design, incorporating cherubs and flowers. Others, however, were designed by an assortment of modern artists, thus corresponding to the international trends of the modern day in art and design.

Brooch made of black molded glass, Heinrich Hoffmann, Gablonz, circa 1914. The design is Wiener Werkstätte. *(From the Lobmeyr Collection, Vienna)*

Filigree brooch set with a large molded stone, from Gablonz, 1920s. European design had been repeatedly inspired by styles from the Far East and other exotic locales. The Gablonz makers, for example, created a line of stones and beads molded in high relief to resemble carved jade, coral and lapis. In the background are items from the "Ingrid" collection.

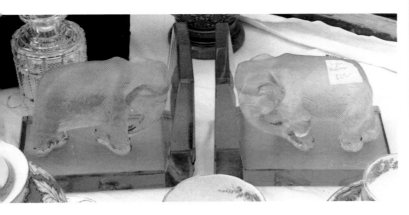

Bookends with elephants, signed H[einrich] Hoffmann, from Gablonz, early 20th century. The elephants were pressmolded in full relief, most likely by the company of Josef Riedel in Polaun. The figures testify to the great talent of the engravers.

One part of the bookends. Naturalistic figures like these were pressmolded in full relief in Gablonz beginning in the mid-19th century; frequently they portrayed famous personalities. Their first success occured around 1880, preceding the Art Deco figurines of the 1920s and 1930s.

This "stone" glass was most carefully finished. Mold seams were cut away and polished, and the surface was given a matte surface by means of an acid treatment. The overall relief was polished, and some areas were cut especially flat and polished, to reveal the delicately shaded inner structure of the glass.

In the following years, Henry G. Schlevogt's efforts in creating new art glass designs were rewarded by such international recognition as the "Grand Prix" at the 1937 Paris World Fair.

Brush and mirror framed with Gürtler-work, backed by molded glass elements, from the "Ingrid" collection by Gablonz's Henry G. Schlevogt, circa 1934. The glass was molded in the Riedel glassworks. Early items from the "Ingrid" collection were, like this one, inspired by Hoffmann designs.

Close-up of the mirror's back, showing the detailed molding, the delicate shading and the careful finish of the malachite green glass.

A modern covered box of molded malachite-green glass from Jablonecké sklarny. The modern items are molded, but are left without further refinement.

Brooch set with a molded stone, from Gablonz, 1920s. Such intricate patterns in high relief required careful engraving and pressmolding. In the background is a box from the "Ingrid" collection.

A close-up of a basket in malachite-green glass from Jablonecké sklarny, 1950s. During this decade, the Czech factory restarted producing various items from the "Ingrid" collection, using either the old molds or the old patterns. These post-war items can be distinguished from the originals by the differences in glass colors and by the sometimes inferior molding quality. In this piece, the relief is rather poor.

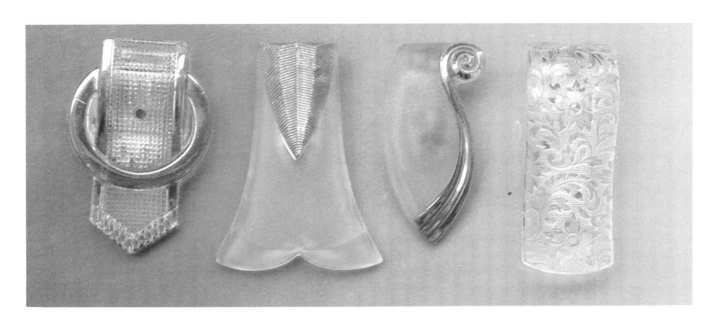

Four molded glass clips, from Gablonz, 1930s. Convincing glass design achieved with simple means.

Two necklaces and two brooches with "jade" and "coral" molded glass stones, from Gablonz, 1920s and 1930s. Opaque stone glass was used consistently in Gablonz from the beginning of the 19th century, though each period saw the rise of different popular designs. The 1920s was dominated by floral patterns in high relief like this one, and by "jade" and "coral" glass.

Bracelet and brooch set with "coral" and "jade" stones. The bracelet is signed "KTF 1935" from Trifari; the brooch is from Gablonz, 1920s/1930s.

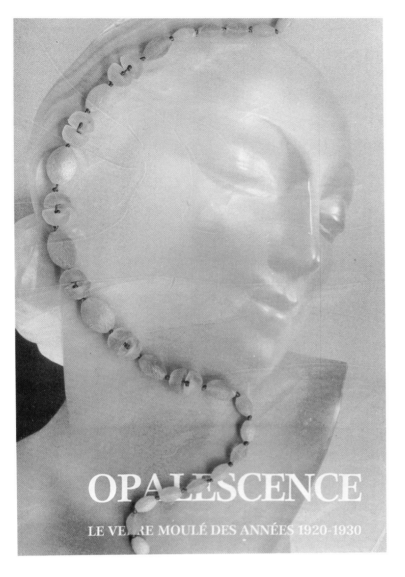

OPALESCENCE

LE VERRE MOULÉ DES ANNÉES 1920-1930

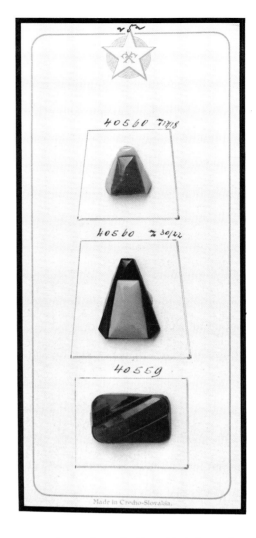

A sample card with molded stones, from the Fried Frères company of Gablonz, late 1920s. Molded designs from Gablonz can come in very varied forms. In this case, two rather plain stones in contrasting colors are assembled into one attractive Art Deco stone.

A necklace composed of delicately molded beads in opalescent and crystal glass, from Gablonz, 1920s. In the background is the cover of a catalogue from the 1986 Brussels exhibition *Opalescence — le verre moule des annees 1920-1930*.

A close-up of the beads from the previous necklace. They are delicate, with a balanced design combining fine opalescent glass with frosted crystal.

A necklace including lampworked beads, from Gablonz, 1930s. The central beads are wound and decorated with a blue and brown thread. The ivory-colored beads on the ends are molded with a knotted pattern corresponding to the metallic knots in the necklace. This piece, with its sophisticated Art Deco design, might well be the product of the Technical School in Gablonz.

A close-up of the stones from the sample card. The molded patterning on some of the stones is extremely delicate and detailed. Molded stones of this caliber generally pass for cut or carved pieces, particularly when they are set in gold or silver mounts.

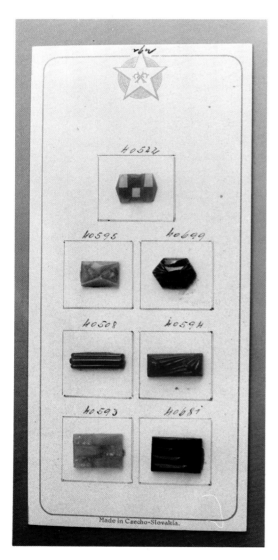

A sample card with molded stones, from the Fried Frères company of Gablonz, late 1920s.

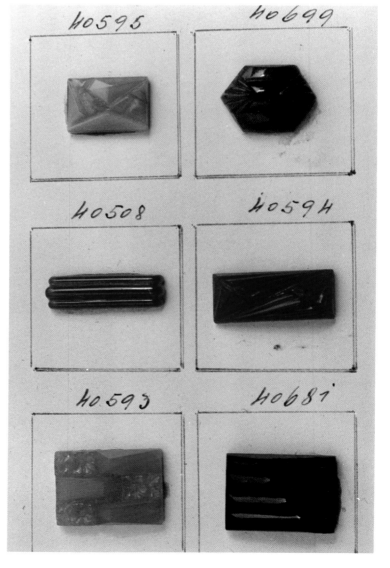

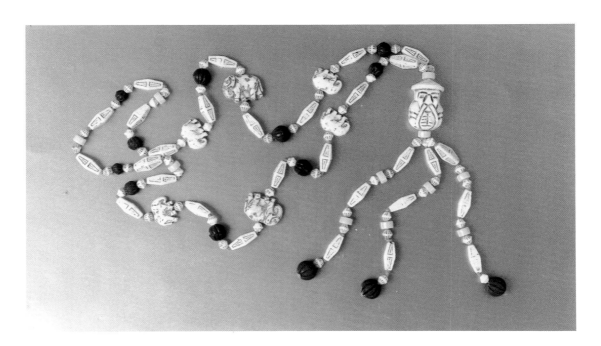

A sample card with molded stones, from the Fried Frères company of Gablonz, late 1920s. The stones are molded of opaque glass imitating natural stones like onyx, lapis and chrysoprase.

A Chinese-style necklace with molded "elephant beads" and a large "Chinese" bead, from Gablonz, 1920s. This style of jewelry often incorporated Asian motifs like this Chinese pattern, and even occasional Indian patterns.

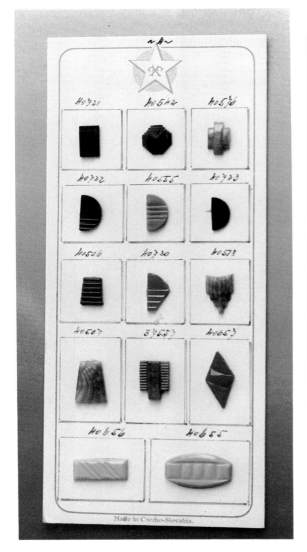

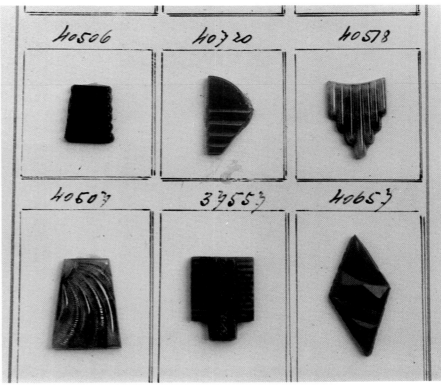

A close-up of the stones on the last sample card. These stones are molded with intricate fancy patterns. Some parts appear to be cut and polished, and other parts seem to be engraved with a delicate flower pattern.

Two strands of molded beads and a pendant with a molded scarab, from Gablonz, 1920s and 1930s. "Egyptian" design like this was inspired by the discovery of Tutenhamen's tomb in 1922. These beads and stones are not among those of highest quality in Gablonz, but they were overwhelmingly successful on the market.

An Egyptian-style necklace with a three-dimensional head, from Gablonz, 19820s. The head, carefully molded with many details, is superior to most other pieces in this genre.

A close-up of the pendant shows the scarab set into a typical and simple Gürtler mount.

A sample card with molded flowers, from the Fried Frères company of Gablonz, late 1920s.

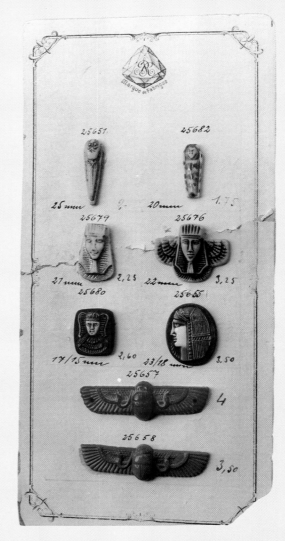

A sample card with various molded stones in Egyptian-style designs, from Gablonz, 1920s/1930s. *(Courtesy of the Museum Warmensteinach)*

Close-up of the molded flowers, revealing the elaborate design of some. The rose flower *(#40566)* or the green flower *(#40567)* even have carefully veined petals.

A sample card with beads and stones in flower shapes, from the Fried Frères company of Gablonz, late 1920s.

Two necklaces with molded flower beads, from Gablonz, circa 1930. The upper necklace included silver-lined beads, while the flowers on the lower necklace are decorated with strass. Both necklaces are composed of simple elements, but are nonetheless charming because of their attractive designs.

Outlook on the Future

An era ended in 1945...but the production of "Gablonz" jewelry continued. The traditions continued in Jablonec, where Czech makers used the infrastructure the Sudetengermans had left behind to make a new start, and in various other locations, primarily in Germany and Austria where the Sudetengermans were finally allowed to settle again. They overcame enormous obstacles to restart their industry.

In the subsequent years, the most important new center developed near Kaufbeuren, in Bavaria, where Gablonzers had already begun production in February 1946. When production began in Neu-Gablonz, the foundation of a wonderful now-47 year old tradition of "Bavarian baubles, buttons and beads" was established.

A flower brooch marked "German - US - Zone," made in Neugablonz, circa 1947. Hope for the future blossomed!

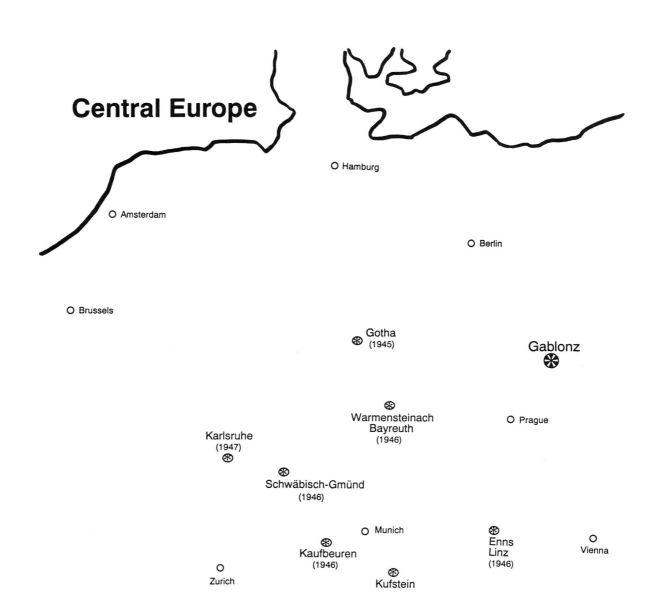

Central Europe

O Hamburg

O Amsterdam

O Berlin

O Brussels

⊛ Gotha
(1945)

Gablonz
✴

⊛
Warmensteinach
Bayreuth
(1946)

O Prague

Karlsruhe
(1947)
⊛

⊛
Schwäbisch-Gmünd
(1946)

O Munich

⊛
Kaufbeuren
(1946)

⊛
Enns
Linz
(1946)

O
Vienna

O
Zurich

⊛
Kufstein

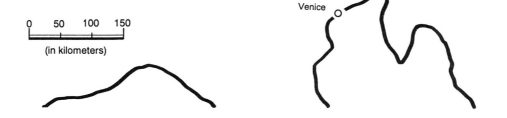

0   50   100   150
(in kilometers)

Venice O

A sketch of the most important places where
Gablonzers settled after World War II to restart
their bijouterie industry.

Endnotes

The People (pp. 5-16)

1 Gordon A. Craig, *The Germans*, London, 1990, Penguin Books, p. 18.
2 Benda, 1877, p. 48.
3 Benda, 1877, p. 49-50.
4 Benda, 1877, p. 297.
5 *Illustrierte Zeitung*, July 23, 1881, p. 817.
6 W. Hopffmann, *Die Geschichte der Juden in Gablonz*, Kaufbeuren-Neugablonz, p. 3.

The Industry (pp. 17-26)

1 Keeß, 1830, p. 696.
2 Kunstgewerbeblatt, 1888, pp. 31-32.

The Glassworks (pp. 27-32)

1 Mittheilungen, 1903, pp. 66-7.

The Composition Makers (pp. 33-36)

1 Benda, 1877, p. 279
2 Zitte, 1958, pp. 101-102.
3 Directory, 1926.
4 Benda, 1877, p. 282.
5 Tayenthal, 1900, p. 7.

Glass Technology (pp. 37-38)

1 Wagner, 1868, p. 371.
2 Sprechsaal, 1876, p. 61.
3 Wieck, 1973, p. 48.

Pressmolding (pp. 49-56)

1 Zitte, 1958, p. 104.
2 Tayenthal, 1900, p. 4.
3 Benda, 1877, p. 294.
4 Benda, 1977, p. 315.

5 Tayenthal, 1900,. p. 247.
6 Kleinert, 1972, p. 25.
7 Leng, 1835, p. 504.
8 Tayenthal, 1900, p. 16.
9 Leng, 1835, p 466.
10 Tayenthal, 1900, p 17.
11 Directory, 1911/12: Rudolf Adolf Weiss, Kukan, No. 274.
12 *Keramische Rundschau*, 1922, pp. 35-6.

Lampworking (pp. 57-64)

1 Keess, 1824, p. 902.
2 Pazaurek, 1911, p. 19.
3 Keess, 1824, p. 903.
4 Keess, 1824, p. 903.
5 Beitrage, 1984, p. 14.

Beads (pp. 65-68)

1 Fischer, 1924, pp. 24-5.
2 Pazaurek, 1911, p. 10.
3 Benda, 1877, p 284.
4 Keeß, 1830, p. 695.
5 Illustrierte Zeitung, 1856, p. 409.
6 Mittheilungen, 1889, p. 62.
7 Wieck, 1878, p. 153.

Buttons (pp. 69-76)

1 Benda, 1877, p. 286.
2 Beitrage, 1984, p. 23.
3 Tayenthal, 1900, p. 257.

Metalworking (pp. 77-104)

1 Rathserlass 1706/07 Bd. 5, p. 157, Staatsarchiv, Nürnberg.
2 Keess, 1824, p. 535.
3 Benda, 1877, p 274.
4 Keess, 1824, p 535.
5 Keess, 1824, p 536.

6 Benda, 1877.
7 Bulletin, 1836, pp. 120-124..
8 Zitte, 1958, p. 51.
9 Zitte, 1958, p 148.
10 Letter by Ernst Seidel, Warmensteinach, October 31, 1990.

Natural Materials (pp. 105-112)

1 Leng, 1835, p. 505.

The Trading Companies (pp. 117-122)

1 Benda, 1877, p. 272.
2 Dingler, 1836, p. 390.
3 Laume/Meier, *Die Allgemeine Industryeausstellung zu Paris*, Leipzig, 1855.
4 Tayenthal, 1900, p. 19.
5 Illustrierte Zeitung, 1856.
6 Sprechsaal, 1878, p. 421.
7 Rousset, 1888, pp. 407-411.
8 Benda, 1877, p. 290.
9 Benda, 1877, p. 288.

The Artistry (p. 128)

1 Fischer, 1914, p 485

Painting & Enameling (pp. 129-134)

1 Zitte, 1958, p. 109.

Satin Glass (pp. 137-142)

1 Sprechsaal, 1870, p. 1004.

Mosaic Glass (pp. 147-148)

1 Zitte, 1958, p. 160.

Bibliography

(Adressbuch 1894):   *Adressbuch der Stadt Gablonz*, Gablonz, 1894

(Adressbuch 1926):   *Adressbuch der Stadt Gablonz*, Gablonz, 1926.

(Balon 1953):   Balon, Erich, *Altgablonz-Neugablonz*, Kaufbeuren, 1953

(Beiträge 1984):   *Beiträge zur Geschichte der Iserbirgler und ihrer Industrie*, No. 5, Schwäbisch-Gmünd, 1984

(Benda 1987):   Benda, Adolf, *Geschichte der Stadt Gablonz und ihrer Umgebung*, Gablonz a.N., 1877

(Bulletin):   *Bulletin de la Société d'encouragement pour l'industrie nationale*, Paris

(Dingler):   *Polytechnisches Journal*, herausgegeben von Dr. Johann Gottfried Dingler, Stuttgart

(Exporteure 1926):   *Verzeichnis der Exporteure in Gablonz a.N.*, Gablonz, 1926

(Fischer 1914):   Fischer, Karl R., Von der Glasindustrie im Iserbirge in: *Deutsche Arbeit* Okt 1913-Sept 1914, Seiten 478-490

(Fischer 1924):   Fischer, Karl R., *Die Schürer von Waldheim*, Prag, 1924

(Glashütte):   *Die Glashütte*, Zeitschrift für die gesamte Glas- und Emailindustrie, Dresden

(Gasparetto 1975):   Gasparetto, Astone, Die Beziehungen zwischen Venedig und Böhmen auf dem Gebiet des Glases zu Beginn des 18. Jahrhunderts, *Glasrevue* 30/1, 1975, Seiten 6-10

(Hannich 1931):   Hannich, Wilhelm, *Die Technik des Glasschmucks*, Leipzig, 1931

(Hohlbaum 1935):   Hohlbaum, Rudolf, Ueber Bijouterieglas in: *Die Glashütte*, Dresden, 1935

(Keess 1824):   Keess, Stephan Ritter von, *Darstellung des Fabriks–und Gewerbewesens*, Wien, 1824

(Keess 1830):   Keess, Stephan Ritter von, *Systematische Darstellung der neuesten Fortschritte in den Gewerben und Manufacturen*, Wien, 1830

(Kleinert 1952):   Kleinert, Hans, *Die Glasdrückerei in Isergebirge*, Schwäbische-Gmünd, 1972

(Leuch 1822):   *Johann Karl Leuch's Neuestes Handbuch für Fabrikanten*, Band 8, Nürnberg, 1822

(Lieferanten 1924):   *Lieferantenverzeichnis von Gablonz und Umgebung*, Gablonz, 1924

(Markovsky 1955):   Markovsky, Rudolf, *Heimatbuch*, Kaufbeuren, 1955

(Mittheilungen):   *Mittheilungen des Nordböhmischen Gewerbemuseums Reichenberg*

(Parkert 1925):   Parkert, Otto W., *Die Perle und ihre künstliche Erzengung*, Leipzig, 1925

(Parkert 1926):   Parkert, Otto W., *Das Verwachsen der Perlen, Glassteine, Metall- und Kunstmasswaren*, Naunhof/Leipzig, 1926

(Pazaurek 1911):   Pazaurek, Gustav E., *Glasperlen und Perlenarbeiten aus alter und neuer Zeit*, Darmstadt, 1911

(Pisling, 1857):   Theephil Pisling, *Nationalökonomische Briefe aus dem nordöstlichen Böhmen*, Prag, 1857.

(Prediger, 1932):   Wilhelm Prediger, *Entwicklungsgänge der Glasindustrie im Isergebirge*, Morchenstern, 1932.

(Prechtl):   *Jahrbücher des kaiserlichen königlichen polytechnischen Institutes in Wien*, herausgegeben von Johan Joseph Prechtl, Wien

(Prediger o.J.):   Prediger, Wilhelm, *Glasbroken*, Morchenstern, o.J.

(Pittrof 1989):   Pittrof, Kurt, *Böhmisches Glas in Panorama der Jahrhunderte*, München, 1989

(Reichenberg 1906):   *Die Kaisertage von Reichenberg und Gablonz-zur Erinnerung anden Besuch der deutsche-böhmischen Ausstellung Reichenberg 1906 durch Seine Majestät den Kaiser*, Wien, 1906

(Riedel 1934):   Riedel, Leopold, Glas in der Schmuckindustrie, *Die Glashütte* No. 38 & 39/ 1934

(Riedel 1991):   *Riedel seit 1756–10 Generationen Glasmacher Ausstellung von Riedel-Gläsern im Museum für Glas und Bijouterie, Jablonec n.n. 19.9-27.10.1991*, Jablonec n.N., 1991

(Riesenfeller 1987):   Riesenfeller, Stefan, *Max Winter im alten Osterreich (Zwischen Iser und Neisse, Bilder aus der Glasklein-industrie Nordböhmens)* Wien, 1987

(Rössler 1979):   Rössler, Susanne, *Gablonz Glas und Schmuck*, München 1979

(Rousset 1888):   Rousset, *Annuaire de la Verrerie*, Paris 1888

(Rundschau):   Keramische Rundschau, *Fachzeitschrift für die Porzellan-, Steinzeug-, Steingut-, Töpfer-, Glas- un Emailindustrie*, Berlin

(Salzer 1931):   Salzer, Robert, Die Gablonzer Glas- und Schmuckindustrie in Ihrer gegewärtigen Lage, in: *Die Glashütte* 23.11.1931 Seiten 865-66

(Schaller, 1785):   Jareslaus Schaller, *Topographie des Königreichs Böhmen*, Prag, 1785

(Schebek 1878):   Schebek, Edmund, *Böhmens Glasindustrie und Glashandel*, Prag, 1878

(Sprechsaal):   Sprechsaal, *Organ der Porzellan-, Glas- und Thornwaarenindustrie*, Coburg

(Stahl 1926):   Stahl, C.J., *Die Glasdruckerei*, Dresden, 1926

(Swarovski 1962):   *Die Geheimnisse Seines Erfolges, Werkszeitung der Swarovskiwerke*, Dezember 1962

(Tagliapietra 1991):   Tagliapietra, Silvano, *Del Presunto viaggio di Guiseppe Briatti in Boemia* (lecture held at the AIHV conference in August 1991 in Vienna)

(Tayenthal. 1900):   Tayenthal, Max v., *Die Gabloner Industrie*, Tübingen und Leipzig, 1900

(Thomas 1982):   *Die Gründung von Betrieben der Gablonzer Industrie im Fichtelgebirge*, Schwäbisch-Gmünd, 1982

(Wagner):   Wagner, Johannes Rudolf, J*ahresbericht über die Fortschritte und Leistungen der chemischen Technologie*, Leipzig

(Wieck):   Friedrich Georg Wiecks, *Deutsche Illustrierte Gewerbezeitung*, Berlin

(Zasche 1900):   Zasche, Adolf, *Das Beizen von Gablonzer Gürtlerwaren*, Gablonz, 1900

(Zenkner 1983):   Zenkner, Karl, *Die Gablonzer Glas- und Schmuckwaren-industrie*, Schwäbisch-Gmünd, 1983

(Zenkner 1968):   Zenkner, Karl, *Die alten Glashütten des Isergebirges*, Schwäbisch-Gmünd, 1983

(Zitte 1958):   Zitte, Rudolf, *Geschichte der Gablonzer Schmuckindustrie*, Neugablonz, 1958

(Zitte/Kleinert):   *Die Entwicklung der Gravierkunst im Isergebirge Die Genossenschaft der Graveure & Emailleure*, Gablonze o.J., c. 1937.

Price Guide (1993)

These pages are intended to provide general guidelines to Bohemian bijouterie values in today's European market. Keep in mind that many factors can influence the price of a particular item: the city or type of shop in which you find the item, the condition of the item, and the many trends of the collectors' marketplace. While the prices listed for items in this book are a good starting point, your common sense will provide the best guide! The left-hand column indicates the page on which each item is pictured; the center column identifies the piece itself. The right-hand column gives the price or price range in Pounds Sterling (£).

page	item	price (Pounds Sterling)	page	item	price
14	necklaces	£ 20-30		bracelet, KTF	25-50
17	shirt buttons	10-20		necklaces	20-40
18	beadwork	10-15		pendant	20-30
20	brooch	10-15		brooch	25-35
21	necklace	15-25	46	button	5-10
	brooch	10-15	47	buttons, 1930s	1-3
22	buttons	2-5		buttons, 19th c.	3-5
	pendant	10-15		mounted cameo	30-50
	brooch	10-15		cameo stone	10-15
23	handle	5-10	49	button	5-10
	necklaces	15-25	50	buttons, 19th c.	3-5
	bracelets	8-12	51	buttons, 1930s	1-3
	brooch	20-50	52	brooch	10-15
24	pendants	25-50		elements for clasp	5-15
	bracelet	10-20		brooch	20-40
25	brooch	15-25		chain	40-60
	clip	10-15	53	cameo, c. 1880	100-150
	clasp	10-15		cameo, 19th c.	100-150
26	bowl	10-20		cameo, Neugablonz	20-35
	bottle	40-60	55	"Amethyst" cameo	100-150
	necklace	15-25		cameo Gablonz	10-20
	ring	10-20		cameo Linz	10-12
	clip	5-10		two cameos	15-20
	pendant	5-10		cameo	15-20
30	perfume set	30-60	56	black cameo (glass)	15-25
31	ink set	50-80		cameo (plastic)	10-15
	segment vases	50-80		white cameo (glass)	10-15
32	buckle brooch	100-150		cameo (plastic)	10-15
	clasps	20-40		set of pins	100-150
34	necklaces	10-12	58	hatpin	10-15
35	necklaces	15-30	59	watch chain	20-30
36	necklaces	15-30		ear pendants	5-10
38	beaker	15-25	60	necklace	15-25
41	ornament	10-15		brooch	10-12
	necklace	15-25		bouquet brooches	5-10
42	necklace	20-30	61	necklace	15-25
	necklace	20-30	62	pendant	10-20
	brooch	10-20		brooches	15-25
43	clips	5-15	63	button	5-10
	brooches	10-20		brooch	10-20
44	handbag	15-20		pendant	10-20
45	necklace, KTF	40-70		brooch	5

68	table mats	5-10
69	buttons	2-5
70	buttons	3-5
72	buttons	2-5
73	green buttons	3-8
	fancy buttons	3-6
	black buttons	1-3
74	fancy buttons	3-6
	plastic buttons	3-5
	buttons, 1930s	1-3
75	buttons, 1930s	1-3
76	metal buttons	2-3
	strass buttons	1-2
	paperweight buttons	5-15
77	brooch	15-25
78	flower brooch	20-25
	bird brooch	10-15
	three brooches	5-15
	grape brooches	5-10
82	belt buckle	20-30
83	two heart brooches	5-15
	portrait pin	3-8
	portrait pendant	3-8
	necklace	20-30
85	three necklaces	15-25
	set, 1930s	20-30
	earclips, 1970s	5-10
86	three bracelets	25-40
88	two brooches	15-25
	belt buckle	10-20
89	Neiger brooch	25-35
90	Nieger pendant	20-40
	brooch	15-20
91	Neiger pendant	20-40
	brooch	2-5
	enameled pendant	30-50
92	oval brooch	20-30
	Neiger brooch	25-40
	Neiger clips	15-25
	Neiger brooch	20-25
93	circular brooch	20-40
	oblong brooch	20-25
	oval brooch	20-35
94	"filigree" brooch	30-50
	two "filigree" clips	10-15
	pendant	15-30
95	brooch	15-25
	buckle brooch	100-150
	brooch	5-10
	clasp	5-10
99	pendant	15-25
	clip	10-15
	oval brooch	20-40
	bangle bracelet	20-40
100	necklace	20-40
	small clip	5-10
	Art Deco necklace	20-40
	green clip	10-15
	brooch	20-30
101	silver pendant	5-10
	Art Deco necklace	20-40
	small clip	5-10
102	dragonfly brooch	20-30
	spider brooch with strass	20-30
	blue spider brooch	20-30

	Ettel spider brooch	10-15
103	butterfly brooch	15-30
	Müller brooch	10-15
	two butterfly brooches	10-20
	Gablonz butterfly brooch	10-20
	Weiss butterfly brooch	20-50
104	two butterfly brooches	15-30
	butterfly clasp	10-20
	insect brooch	15-25
	butterfly brooches	10-25
106	two wooden watch chains	5-15
	necklace	10-15
107	necklace	10-15
	purse	5-10
	four necklaces	15-30
	vase	50-100
108	three vases	20-40
109	studs	10-15
	paperweight brooch	20-30
	dog brooch	10-20
	rose brooch	25-50
110	long necklace	25-50
	brooch	5
	belt buckle	5
111	three clips	5-15
	clip	10-15
	necklace	20-30
112	two necklaces	15-25
	bracelet	10-15
	two brooches	10-15
	celluloid fan	15-20
113	bangle bracelet	10-15
114	necklace w/carved beads	15-20
	long necklace	20-35
115	two long necklaces	20-30
	necklace w/carved beads	15-25
	long spider necklace	25-35
116	long red necklace	30-40
	two Art Deco necklaces	20-25
118	ink bottle	30-50
	paperweight	25-40
120	two jet brooches	5-15
	cameo Gablonz	15-25
	cameo in gold mount	200-250
123	two mosaic brooches	20-30
	golden brooch	30-40
	square brooch	20-30
126	filigree bangles	5
	enameled bangles	5-10
127	striped bangles	5-10
	fancy mirror bangles	10-20
	decorated bangles	10-20
	necklace	20-40
128	paperweight	50-80
129	portrait button	15-30
	violet brooch	15-30
	handpainted buttons	2-5
130	pinted brooch	10-15
	pinted pendant	15-20
	enameled brooch	15-25
	"Mary Gregory" brooch	—
131	iris belt buckle	25-40
	mosaic clasp	10-20
	enameled brooch	20-50
	enameled pendant	15-25

	enameled brooches	20-50
132	enameled brooches	20-30
	leather handbag	30-50
	enameled frame handbag	40-60
133	two scarf holders	15-30
	three enameled brooches	20-25
	enameled Art Deco clasp	10-20
	souvenir brooch	10
134	bi-colored vase	10-15
	ruby-flashed earrings	10-15
	ruby-flashed paperweight	50-100
	bi-colored necklaces	20-30
135	cut overlay vase	100-150
	four necklaces	15-30
136	brooch	80-120
137	two enameled brooches	20-50
	two satin glass brooches	15-20
	satin glass necklace	20-30
138	large satin glass brooch	15-25
	small satin glass brooch	10-15
	satin glass clasp	15-25
	satin glass brooch	15-25
	enameled pendant	20-30
139	saphiret brooch	10-15
	saphiret necklace	30-50
	three saphiret pendants	25-50
	silver button brooch	10-15
140	three small saphiret brooches	15-25
	two saphiret brooches	20-30
	saphiret button	5-10
	saphiret brooch	10-15
	"rhinestone" brooch	10-15
141	four "rhinestone" pendants	15-30
	three "rhinestone" brooches	10-15
	three "rhinestone" necklaces	15-30
142	fancy glass brooch	10-20
	fancy glass clasp	15-25
	"peloton" vase	80-120
143	three buttons	3-5
	vase	20-40

	brooch	20-40
144	"opal" brooch	10-15
	two aventurine brooches	40-80
	vase w/mica flecks	30-50
145	two necklaces	25-35
	necklace	25-35
	silver brooch w/cabochon	40-60
146	belt buckle and element	50-80
	silver brooch	30-60
	paperweight	150-250
149	brooch	30-50
151	black buttons	2-5
	jet bijouterie	20-30
152	necklace	15-20
154	green brooch	15-20
	brooch w/marcasite pattern	15-20
	clasp w/cabochons	15-20
	carnelian-colored clasp	20-25
	five clips	5-10
155	clasp w/yellow satin glass	15-25
	bronze clasp	15-20
	red clasp	15-20
156	red buttons	1-3
	red clasp	15-20
	coral-colored clasp	15-20
157	filigree brooch	20-30
158	brush & mirror set	60-150
159	covered box	5
	brooch	15-25
	glass basket	30-40
160	four clips	5-10
	two necklaces	25-35
	large brooch	25-40
	small brooch	10-15
	bracelet, KTF	25-50
	brooch	10-15
161	necklace	20-40
162	necklace	20-30
163	necklace	30-40
164	necklace	30-40
	pendant	10-20
166	two necklaces	20-30

Index